D0205409

# JENNIFER JONES

*Portrait of Jennie* (1948). Courtesy of the Billy Rose Theatre Collection, New York Public Library at Lincoln Center, Astor, Lenox, and Tilden Foundations.

# JENNIFER JONES

## *A Bio-Bibliography*

Jeffrey L. Carrier

Bio-Bibliographies in the Performing Arts, Number 11
James Robert Parish, Series Adviser

**Greenwood Press**
New York • Westport, Connecticut • London

PN
2287
J59
C37
1990

**Library of Congress Cataloging-in-Publication Data**

Carrier, Jeffrey L.
   Jennifer Jones : a bio-bibliography / Jeffrey L. Carrier.
      p.   cm.—(Bio-bibliographies in the performing arts, ISSN
   0892-5550 ; no. 11)
   ISBN 0-313-26651-4 (lib. bdg. : alk. paper)
   1. Jones, Jennifer, 1919-  . 2. Jones, Jennifer, 1919-   —
Bibliography. 3. Actors—United States—Biography. I. Title.
II. Series.
PN2287.J59C37   1990
791.43'028'092—dc20        89-25834

British Library Cataloguing in Publication Data is available.

Library of Congress Catalog Card Number: 89-25834
ISBN: 0-313-26651-4
ISSN: 0892-5550

First published in 1990

Greenwood Press, 88 Post Road West, Westport, CT   06881
An imprint of Greenwood Publishing Group, Inc.

Printed in the United States of America

∞

The paper used in this book complies with the
Permanent Paper Standard issued by the National
Information Standards Organization (Z39.48-1984).

10 9 8 7 6 5 4 3 2 1

For Bub

# Contents

# Illustrations

# *Preface*

I'll never forget seeing my first Jennifer Jones movie. Even now, nearly ten years after that late night in a college dorm when there was nothing else to do but watch television, the memory of her in *Portrait of Jennie* remains vivid and unforgettable.

As the otherworldly ghost, she cast a spell over me so potent that it still remains my favorite Jones film and performance, her Oscar-winning portrayal of Bernadette Soubirous included. The movie is surely one of the most romantic ever made, and its message that Love is timeless, that even two people from different eras can find eternal happiness together, struck such a responsive chord in me that for days I walked around in a romantic stupor.

It surprised me to later learn that the film had been neither well-received by critics nor successful at the box-office. How could anyone not be simply mad about *Portrait of Jennie*? The photography is appropriately moody, Dimitri Tiomkin's score is hauntingly romantic and the acting is superb. Lillian Gish and Ethel Barrymore are especially fine, but it is Jennifer Jones, as the ethereal, innocently romantic ghost, who impresses most.

Sadly, the film marked a turning point in her career, a career which had begun inauspiciously in 1939 when, using the name Phylis Isley (her own), she appeared in a minor western and a Dick Tracy serial at Republic. As Jennifer Jones (a Selznick contractee) she won an Oscar for her first important film, *Song of Bernadette* (1943), and received fine reviews and additional nominations for *Since You Went Away* (1944), *Love Letters* (1945), and *Duel in the Sun* (1946). Critics also found her delightful in Ernst Lubitsch's funny *Cluny Brown*, also 1946, but something went wrong with *Portrait of Jennie*. She was as good as ever, but the film left the critics strangely unmoved. Shot in 1947, producer David O. Selznick held up its release for nearly two years while he tried to turn the gentle love story into a near-epic by adding a pretentious prologue (narrated by Ben Hecht) and expanding the storm climax into a wide-screened, sepia-toned hurricane. It did not work. The story is a fragile and delicate one and his tinkering only succeeded in throwing the film off balance. But despite his meddling, *Portrait of Jennie*'s reputation is gaining ground with  film scholars and students.

The film was released in 1949, the same year she and Selznick were married, following several years of a not-so-secret romance. They had met in 1941, when, as a young New York housewife named Phylis Walker, with two small sons, some radio and stage experience (she didn't mention her failed try to make it in the movies) and a strong desire to act, she auditioned for the leading role in *Claudia*.  The film rights to Rose Franken's play (a Broadway success with Dorothy McGuire) had been bought by Selznick and although Mrs. Walker lost the part, an impressed Selznick signed her to a contract anyway, changed her name to Jennifer Jones, launched her to stardom in *Song of Bernadette* and gradually fell in love with his young discovery. Her marriage to Robert Walker (whom she had married in 1939, and who was signed by MGM  in 1943) quickly fell apart, as did Selznick's marriage to Irene Mayer, daughter of MGM boss L.B.

*Song of Bernadette* was to be 20th Century-Fox's most prestigious film of 1943, and their "unknown" star was publicized as being almost as saintly as Bernadette herself. Her marriage and motherhood were kept quiet for a while, the producers concerned as to what would happen if the public found out that sweet, young, virginal Bernadette was married and the mother of two children.  The story finally leaked, but the problem was solved by playing up the "happy young couple in love" angle. They were affectionately called "Mr. and Mrs. Cinderella" and their marriage was considered idyllic, but even before *Bernadette* premiered, they separated (the reasons for which were not made public), and when she announced the day after she won her Oscar that she had filed for divorce, Hollywood was shocked. How could Bernadette degrade herself that way? Respected columnist Adela Rogers St. Johns finally pleaded her case, writing that Jennifer had a life of her own and could not be expected to dedicate that life to the spirit of a girl who had lived so long ago, but a great deal of sympathy went out to Robert Walker who was so obviously in love with his wife. He never seemed to recover from the blow and grew increasingly moody and disturbed, suffering a series of nervous breakdowns.  He died in 1951 from respiratory failure, probably induced from drugs administered to quieten another of his emotional outbursts.  He was 33 years old.

In the midst of this marriage controversy, *Song of Bernadette* was released to the neighborhood theatres during the summer of 1944 (it had premiered in December, 1943, in Los Angeles) and became one of the year's biggest moneymakers.

If Jennifer's saintly image was badly shaken by the 1945 divorce, it was shattered forever when she made *Duel in the Sun* for Selznick the following year.  Her portrayal of half-breed Pearl Chavez was -- up to that time -- one of the most searingly carnal personifications of sexuality ever seen on the screen. The film was jokingly referred to as "lust in the dust," and although her performance did merit another Oscar nomination, the film pleased Selznick (who, according to witnesses, stood off camera and panted during the shooting of Jennifer's sensual scenes) more than the critics.

The gossip columnists were delighted by their marriage, which they had been predicting for two years, terming it a great love story. Many have tried to analyze Jones's attraction and marriage to Selznick, a man 17 years older than she, and a man not considered particularly handsome. Jennifer, who has always seemed shy and insecure in articles and interviews, perhaps needed (or wanted) the attention and love of a powerful man, and decided to abandon her marriage to Walker, a sensitive actor who was as timid and insecure as she was, but most feel that it was solely for the sake of her career, that power was more attractive than love. Whatever the case may be -- and it isn't likely that she will ever tell -- as the wife of one of the most powerful producers in Hollywood, she *did* have an inordinate amount of attention lavished upon her career. Films were carefully chosen for her, with Selznick usually producing, but even when not actively involved in the production, he would still inundate the director with lengthy memos dictating how his wife should be directed, photographed and costumed.

Unfortunately, Selznick's keen judgment, responsible for such classics as *Little Women* (1933), *Gone With the Wind* (1939) and *Rebecca* (1940), had seemingly diminished. Many of these films were unsuccessful with Jones often receiving poor reviews (excepting the phenomenally popular *Love is a Many-Splendored Thing*, 1955, which earned her a fifth Oscar nomination). The failure of the expensive *A Farewell to Arms* (1957) ended Selznick's career and dealt Jennifer a severe blow as well.

She had made only one additional film, the ill-received *Tender is the Night* (1961), when Selznick died in 1965, at the age of 62. A few months following his death she flew to London to take over for an ill Kim Stanley in *The Idol*, but neither she nor the film were much liked. After two years of silence, she was suddenly news again after an unsuccessful suicide attempt in 1967. She has never publicly explained why she walked into the ocean under the cliffs of Malibu that late November night (some said she couldn't cope with the loneliness after Selznick's death; others thought it was the guilt of knowing she may have caused the unhappiness Walker suffered after their divorce), but whatever the reason, she was pulled from the surf to make two more films and marry for a third time. She wed canned-food millionaire and art collector Norton Simon in 1971, and during the past 19 years has devoted herself to charities and to serving as Chairman of the Norton Simon Museum in Pasadena, which houses the largest private collection of paintings in the world. She was last seen on the big screen in 1974 as part of *The Towering Inferno*'s all-star cast, and despite purchasing the film rights to *Terms of Endearment* in the late 70's, she later sold them and seems now to have little interest in making another film.

Jennifer Jones is unquestionably an important part of film history; several of her screen performances were critically acclaimed, she avoided type-casting and had a large public following, but less careful handling by Selznick (she didn't get the opportunity to develop a talent for comedy that Lubitsch uncovered in *Cluny Brown*) might have made her a more credible screen performer for a longer period of time; however, as it stands, the film career of Jennifer Jones (23 features and one serial in 35 years) is a long and distinguished one. But had she made only *Portrait of Jennie*, her touching portrayal of the lonely, fey ghost would be remembered as long as there are film buffs, revival houses and romantics.

* * *

This book is not intended to be a fully developed or intimate biography, rather it is a research tool for those interested in an academic study of the career of Jennifer Jones, an actress whose performances are badly in need of re-evaluation. She is an actress rarely thought of as an individual, but only as a puppet whose strings were rigidly controlled by David O. Selznick, and although it was he who discovered her, made her a star, married her and spent years trying to elevate her to the ranks of a cinema immortal/love goddess, she remained very much an individual actress with a unique style. Selznick failed in his attempt to make her a screen immortal, and it is often *she* who is blamed by critics who claim she didn't have the talent to support Selznick's faith and grandiose plan. (Some of her performances *were* surprisingly poor, lending some credence to that opinion.)

Jennifer is also usually held responsible for the mental collapse of Robert Walker after their divorce. This seems rather unfair. Of course, both were close-mouthed about the divorce and what really happened may never be known, but lots of husbands have lost their wives to other men. It happens all the time -- especially in Hollywood -- and most of them manage to remain sane. Is it not possible that Walker was slightly off-balance *before* the marriage, and the divorce was merely the proverbial straw that broke the camel's back? Jennifer Jones is often pictured as a grasping, gold-digging woman who married Selznick solely for the advancement of her career. It's likely; however, not often mentioned is the fact that, as Selznick's wife, she remained loyal to him until his death, and also, from all accounts, has been a faithful wife to Norton Simon.

This book looks at Jennifer Jones as Jennifer Jones, not as Selznick's protegee and wife, or even as the woman who divorced Robert Walker. By separating her performances from the Selznick influence and examining them on their own merit, her talent is often surprising. Naturally, Selznick and Walker are included, but it is Jennifer Jones who is the star of this study.

The book is divided into seven major sections:
1) A detailed biography.
2) A chronology that summarizes the highlights of her life.
3) A complete filmography that also includes selected reviews, additional sources for research on each film, and author's notes.
4) A listing of her radio, theatre and television appearances.
5) Awards and nominations
6) An annotated bibliography that includes references in books, magazines and newspapers.

7)  An index of all names, film titles and corporate names.

The   New York Times obituaries of Robert Walker and David O. Selznick  are also reprinted in an appendix.

For a more intimate biography of Jennifer Jones (one that includes more information of her marriages to Walker and Selznick), I recommend Beverly Linet's *Star-Crossed*, G.P. Putnam's Sons, 1986.

# Acknowledgments

There are many people without whose support and assistance this book would not have been possible. First and foremost, I must thank Marilyn Brownstein for taking the time to read and respond to sample chapters and seemingly inconsequential questions, and for graciously extending my deadline, and James Parish for his advice and support. Others to whom I am forever grateful include William K. Everson, Karen Latham Everson, Rick DeCroix, Bill Klein, Doug McClelland, Joe Desiderio, Mary Corliss and her assistant, Terri Geeskin, at the Museum of Modern Art Film Stills Archive, the staff of the New York Public Library at Lincoln Center, and Don at the Library of Congress who responded to my phone query. Lastly, I thank my father, Rev. Ed Carrier, who has never failed to believe in me and give me support when I needed it most.

*1*

# Biography: A Portrait of Jennifer

It was inevitable that Jennifer Jones would become an actress. From the moment she was born she knew nothing other than acting. It was her parents' livelihood.

Phil and Flora Mae Suber Isley were the owners, operators and stars of the Isley Stock Company, an acting troup that toured the south central states from a base in Tulsa, Oklahoma, where their only child -- a daughter -- was born on Sunday, March 2, 1919. She was named Phylis Lee.

The Isleys and their troup of vaudeville-trained actors toured during the summers, pitching their tents outside cities and towns and charging patrons a dime to see such old favorites as *East Lynne* and *The Old Homestead*. Sometimes Phil would give the audience an extra treat, a slide show of New York City's Chinatown, complete with his warnings of the evil therein, although he had actually never seen the place.

Phylis, a pretty child with dark eyes and wavy dark hair, trouped right along with the rest of the company, soaking up the exciting backstage environment, and by the time she was six, she had already made it her life's ambition to be an actress. Her parents weren't really surprised, but were a little concerned about the acute shyness she had developed, and to help her overcome this affliction -- not particularly conducive to an acting career -- Phil made her an official member of the staff. By the time she was ten, she was taking tickets, selling candy and making herself generally useful. Occasionally she would play a juvenile part, but her stage bow was not with her parents' company, but at the Edgemere Public School in Oklahoma City, where she appeared as a peppermint stick in a Christmas play.

Unlike some stock company proprietors, the Isleys made money. Phil was a good manager. He not only made sure that his family had every comfort and that his daughter attended good schools, but that something was put away for the future when times might not be so good.

As it turned out, he was wise. During Phylis's tenth year, the stock market crashed, but this gave Phil a unique opportunity. Many of the independent movie theatres -- those not owned by major film companies --

were left in poor financial condition.  Silent movies had been supplanted by the new "talkies," and without the means to install sound equipment, these independent movie houses faced bankruptcy.  Isley had the cash, so he bought the theatres, equipped them for sound, and in a fairly short time became rather well-to-do with his small chain of Oklahoma/Texas movie theatres.

Phylis was particularly excited by her father's business and became a regular moviegoer.  The desire to act, temporarily dormant, was vigorously renewed and she would return from the movies aping the mannerisms of deep-voiced Sylvia Sidney and theatrical Helen Hayes.  She also became fond of reading plays, her favorite being *The Barretts of Wimpole Street*, Rudolph Besler's love story of English poets Robert and Elizabeth Barrett Browning.

Phylis graduated from grade school in 1932 and was enrolled in Tulsa's Mounte Cassino Junior College, a private school of the Benedictine Sisters.  During her four years there she seemed to lose some of her shyness; she made close friends, joined a girls club and had the lead in most of the school plays.  As she neared graduation, she decided her place was on the stage, but wasn't sure how to get there.  Writing her idol, stage great Katherine Cornell, she asked if it was best to get a college education or attend a dramatic school before attempting the stage.  Miss Cornell's quick reply recommended a "cultural background."

Phylis had become a five-foot-seven beauty by the time of her 1936 graduation.  She was voted May Queen, but turned down the title of class valedictorian, letting a close friend have the honor. Confident of his daughter's abilities, Phil tried to convince Phylis to go to Hollywood -- he had connections -- but no doubt thinking of Katherine Cornell's advice, she announced her plans to attend Northwestern University.  The university's drama department was well known and Phylis thought that if she was to become a serious actress, she'd better try to learn as much about the profession as she could.  Phil broke down and agreed to pay her tuition, and in September, 1936, she entered the freshman class as a drama major.

Her year at Northwestern was not a happy one; the summer stock experience put her miles ahead of her drama classmates, and the non-acting courses bored her.  The only bright spot was a Christmas trip with her parents to New York where she finally saw her beloved Katherine Cornell in *Wingless Victory* five times.  The acting bug bit even harder, and by spring term's end, she had definitely made up her mind to attend New York's Academy of Dramatic Arts (AADA), and had no trouble convincing her father to pay the tuition.

With his confidence in Phylis unshaken, Phil arranged for her to be engaged by the Mansfield Players, a summer stock company, as their leading lady for their summer tour of the southwest.  Phylis gladly accepted the job and performed capably in such chestnuts as *The Family Upstairs* and *This Thing Called Love*, although her favorite role was Moonyean in *Smilin' Through*.  When the tour ended, she considered herself ready to go before the Academy's admission judges.

Enacting a scene from *Wingless Victory*, 18-year-old Phylis Isley auditioned on September 10, 1937. The admission judges found her "promising," with an "attractive personality, a good stage presence, an above-average voice, a sensitive temperament and a definite dramatic instinct." (See source no. B023) She passed. Mr. and Mrs. Isley, who had accompanied their daugher to New York, saw that she was safely boarded at the Barbizon Hotel for Women on Lexington Avenue at 63rd Street, then wished her well and headed back to Oklahoma.

Phylis devoted herself to her classes, making little time for social activities, but that changed on January 2, 1938, when, upon her return after Christmas break, she met fellow student Robert Walker.

A native of Utah, he had come to AADA by way of the Army and Naval Academy in San Diego where he had excelled in dramatics. The two acted in skits together, talked together between classes and spent their free time on long walks and aboard the Staten Island ferry where you could ride to nowhere for a nickel. Soon they were inseparable, and in love.

When spring came, it was time to audition again before the judges, those members of the faculty who decided if first year students would be invited back for another term. Phylis had lost none of her fondness for *The Barretts of Wimpole Street*, and although Walker didn't consider himself a Robert Browning type, he agreed to perform an excerpt from the play with her. They were both invited back for the fall term.

Phil Isley had engaged his daughter for another summer of stock, and it was no doubt a tearful parting at New York's Penn Station as the two young, much-in-love, would-be actors embraced, kissed probably, and promised to be true to each other during the long, long summer ahead.

So Phylis returned to dusty Oklahoma and the hot canvas of summer stock tents, leaving Walker behind to find odd jobs. She trouped from town to town with the Mansfield Players and the Harley Sadler Players, no doubt giving good performances, but when not memorizing her lines, her mind was probably on the shy, sensitive boy from Utah who was waiting for her return to New York. What she didn't know was that Walker wasn't having it so easy. He had tried to find odd jobs, but none lasted, and a cheap meal in a dockside diner led to his joining the crew of a banana boat.

Sometime during that summer of 1938, while Walker was helping transport bananas from South America to New York, staring right into the face of life's seamier side, he decided not to return to the Academy in the fall, but to try to find stage work. Why was he studying to be an actor when he already was one?

When Phylis returned from Oklahoma, fresh from new acting challenges, ready to resume her classes at the Academy and hone her talents even more, Walker was at the train station to meet her. He expected the worst when he told Phylis his plans, and it is a testament of her love for him that she decided not to return to school either, but to accompany him on the search for stage jobs. And so they made the rounds, leaving 8 x 10 glossies with every casting director in town, hoping for even a small break. But no one was willing to give them one.

One day they happened to hear about Paul Gilmore and his Cherry Lane Theatre in Greenwich Village, where young, non-equity actors could perform and hopefully be seen by theatrical agents and scouts. They went to see this Mr. Gilmore, who welcomed them into the fold and agreed to pay them fifty cents each per performance. It wasn't the job they had hoped for-- the theatre was old and they had to share dressingrooms with mice -- but they were acting, and they were together, and wasn't that all that really mattered?

Phylis had told her parents of her decision not to return to the Academy, and although they couldn't convince her to change her mind, they did insist that she remain at the Barbizon. They also promised to send her a weekly allowance, but they considered her decision to leave school an impetuous one and were soon on their way to New York to see how their daughter was faring. And what they found disturbed them: the dingy theatre, the less than sufficient income and the long walk home after each night's performance, a good two miles on the not-so-safe streets of New York. Walker accompanied Phylis to the Barbizon each evening, then walked back to Beekman where he shared an apartment with his brother, but the Isleys were not happy with their daughter's situation. When they returned to Tulsa, they arranged for a radio station there to offer Phylis the tempting job of starring in her own weekly dramatic program for 13 weeks, at twenty-five dollars per week. She responded by saying she would accept *only* if Walker was hired as her leading man at a matching salary. He was, so they left the Cherry Lane Theatre in November and headed for Tulsa where *The Phylis Isley Radio Theatre* was soon heard over station KOME every Sunday afternoon. They were still acting, and still together.

It isn't documented when Phylis Isley and Robert Walker became engaged (one source has them considering marriage even before the end of the Academy's spring term, another that Walker proposed on a bench in Central Park the day Phylis returned from Oklahoma), but they were certainly planning it by this time, and much of their combined weekly salary of fifty dollars was put away with a wedding in mind. The Isleys, at first underwhelmed by Walker, eventually came to appreciate him almost as much as their daughter did.

Phylis and Bob were married on January 2, 1939, the anniversary of their first meeting, with Phylis wearing a red velvet dress and peter pannish hat. As a wedding present, the Isleys presented the couple with a new car, and although sources differ as to the color -- some say blue, others say red -- all agree that it was a convertible and brand new.

The 13-week contract with KOME had expired so, at Phil Isley's urging, Mr. and Mrs. Robert Walker filled their new car with luggage and headed to California, determined to make it in the movies. They didn't expect simply to stroll through the studio gates and into a leading role; through his theatre chain, Phil still had those Hollywood connections, and they were optimistic that finding work in Hollywood would be easier than it had been in New York.

After a brief stopover in Utah, where Phylis met her inlaws, they arrived in California, the golden land of opportunity, with four hundred dollars and Phil Isley's letters of introduction. A boarding house on LaBrea Avenue was near the major studios and the rent fit nicely into their budget, so they moved in and began their search for work. They tried Paramount first, and, relying on their artistic training at AADA, chose to enact a scene from Ibsen's *Ghosts* in which Phylis played her husband's *mother*. Their heavy emoting didn't impress the casting directors and although they were turned down, they refused to be discouraged; there were other studios. But when summer came and still they had no work, and with their savings running low, they put aside their pride, pulled out Phil's last letter of introduction, and went to Republic, at that time one of the least respected studios in Hollywood. Republic specialized in low budget westerns and quickie serials, and although Walker wasn't their type, they found Phylis appealing and signed her to the basic six-month contract at seventy-five dollars per week.

She was assigned a film role almost immediately -- the love interest in a Three Mesquiteer western with John Wayne. Titled *New Frontier*, the plot pitted rugged ranchers against evil businessmen who planned to turn a valley into a reservoir and gave Phylis little opportunity to act. Director George Sherman later recalled that she "seemed to have much more talent than her role called for. When not working, she took in every phase of the filming technique, which was obviously new to her." (See source no. B030)

Her work on the film was completed within five days and she was then cast as Gwen Andrews, the secretary in the fifteen-chapter serial, *Dick Tracy's G Men*. Although she appeared in thirteen episodes, her spoken dialogue added up to a mere 204 words, and her salary for the five days of filming, including overtime, totalled a mere $90.62.

Walker had been able to get nothing more than a couple of bit parts, and he and Phylis soon realized that making it in the movies wasn't as easy as they expected. Discouraged and disappointed, they decided to return to New York, and Phylis asked to be released from her contract. This might have been a problem, but through her father's influence (Isley Theatres were an important outlet for Republic's films), this was done without objection. With their ties to Hollywood severed, the young couple sold their car for one thousand dollars, climbed aboard a New York bound train and didn't look back.

They arrived in New York with renewed enthusiasm. It was autumn, when casting on Broadway was at its peak, and with their now-impressive resumes, they thought they couldn't fail. They saved money by moving into a cold water flat on West Tenth Avenue and made the rounds every day. Hoping for a chance, they got nothing but rejections, and by winter their savings had sunk as low as their spirits. Although Phylis did find occasional work modelling millinery for the John Robert Powers Agency, pregnancy soon forced her to give that up.

As the baby's arrival drew nearer, they realized the cold, tiny flat was not a proper place for an infant, so they rented a cheap cottage in Long Beach, Long Island, and they had just finished unpacking when Phylis felt the first labor pain. At five a.m. on April 15, 1940, Robert Walker, Jr. was born in Jamaica Hospital, Queens.

The child's birth seemed to bring them luck. Within days, Walker had a job acting on the radio, and in a very short time was working nearly every day in radio soaps. As his career was finally taking off, Phylis's was standing still. Three months after the birth of Bobby, Jr., she was pregant again, and had to be content with staying at home with the baby, listening to her husband on the radio and helping him with lines and characterization when he came home at night. It was frustrating, but she was pleased with her husband's success and was simply marking time until she could resume her own search for an acting job.

Michael Ross Walker was born on March 13, 1941, and the time finally seemed right for Phylis to go back to work. She went to see *Claudia* on stage with Dorothy McGuire and was convinced she would be perfect in the role. The play would soon be opening in Chicago and a search was already underway to find a Chicago Claudia. Through Walker's agent, Phylis managed to be tested for the part by none other than Rose Franken, the play's author, but she lost to another Phyllis -- Phyllis Thaxter.

Plans to film the play were also underway. Producer David O. Selznick, fresh from his *Gone With the Wind* triumph, had bought the film rights for $187,000 and, not sure of Miss McGuire's drawing power, was looking for a film Claudia. Katherine Brown, Selznick's New York agent, learned of Miss Franken's interest in the two Phyllises and arranged to have them read for the part. Phylis Walker's appointment was on July 21, and that visit to Selznick's Fifth Avenue office would change the course of her life.

She had memorized one of her favorite scenes from the play and tried to give a good reading but something happened, and as she would say later, "I was very, very bad." (See source no. B023) She burst into tears, and, thinking she had ruined whatever chance she had, fled from the room. Selznick, who had witnessed the outburst, told his assistant to make an appointment the following day for him to meet personally with the sensitive young woman. Phylis received the message when she got home but ignored it, thinking they only wanted to let her down easily.

When the appointed hour came and Phylis had not arrived at Selznick's office, Miss Brown called to ask where she was. Phylis answered and was told that Mr. Selznick was waiting to see her. She had just shampooed her hair, but she quickly dressed, called a cab and rushed to Manhattan in record time, dangling her wet hair out the window to dry.

Selznick was indeed waiting, but he didn't want her to read again; he merely wanted to chat. She told him of her tent show background, and of her desire to play Claudia, but didn't mention her aborted career at Republic. When she left his office, she wasn't exactly sure what was going to happen, but she hoped it would be something good.

And it was something good; four days later, on July 26, 1941, Phylis Isley Walker signed a personal, seven-year contract with Selznick International. According to the contract, her initial salary would be two hundred dollars per week, but would gradually escalate to the princely sum of three thousand per week by the end of the seventh year.

She hoped to start work immediately, but Selznick kept her idle for weeks, telling her nothing other than she would soon be tested for *Claudia*. Actually, Selznick didn't know what to do with her. He sensed she was star quality, but wanted to find just the right film in which to showcase her; however, something first had to be done about that name. He thought "Phylis Walker" too bland, too undistinguished, and instructed his staff to come up with ideas. Four months later, not satisfied with any of the suggestions, he came up with his own idea, a name which had always been his favorite -- Jennifer. The last name, he said, should be simple, but still blend well with the first name. Someone suggested Jones, and it was settled. In January, 1942, an unknown actress from Oklahoma named Jennifer Jones, was presented to the press as Selznick's newest discovery. Someone asked her how she happened to be named Jennifer, and she said, rather shyly, "My mother must have been reading an English novel." (See source no. B023.)

Before her re-christening, Phylis had been sent to California in August to appear for two weeks in a one-act play at Santa Barbara's Lobrero Theatre. Written by William Saroyan and directed by John Houseman, *Hello, Out There* allowed Selznick to assess her dramatic abilities and gauge audience reaction. The play was presented as a curtain raiser to *The Devil's Disciple* with Alan Marshall and Janet Gaynor, but it was *Hello, Out There*, and specifically Phylis Walker, who stole the notices. Selznick was pleased.

In September, at Selznick's California studio, she finally tested for the title role in *Claudia*. Her screen presence and innocent loveliness surprised even Selznick and in a memo to Rose Franken, he called Phylis a "knock out," but Miss Franken had a great deal of influence as to who would star in the filmization of her play, and she preferred Dorothy McGuire.

When Phylis returned to her husband and sons in late September, she still didn't know when she would begin working, and to ease her boredom, Selznick suggested she take private acting lessons from Sanford Meisner. Boredom wasn't all that was bothering her; she had purposely *not* mentioned her earlier contract to Republic, but knew sharp-eyed film goers might recognize her, exposing Selznick's false publicity that she was "new to films." She mustered her courage and told Selznick everything during one of his frequent trips to New York. Although he told her not to worry, he *did* do some checking to make sure her contract to Republic had indeed been terminated. He feared there might have been a clause preventing her from working for other studios. Thankfully, there wasn't, but months went by and there was still no word as to when she would be given a film role.

At the time of her formal introduction to the press, she was definitely being considered as a possible Nora in *Keys of the Kingdom*, but when Selznick decided to liquidate Selznick International in mid-summer, 1942, to form a smaller company, the film rights to A.J. Cronin's book (along with the other properties owned by Selznick) were sold to 20th Century-Fox. That eliminated the possibility of her being Nora, and the chances of her getting *Claudia* were gone too. Miss Franken was finally able to insist that casting be done her way, and Dorothy McGuire made her screen debut when *Claudia* was filmed in 1943.

Phylis's first year option expired in July, 1942, and despite a year of inactivity, her contract was renewed; however, a new seven-year contract was drawn up on August 15, with the promise that a suitable role would soon be hers. Two more months went by before, in late October, she was suddenly called to the coast to test for the lead in Fox's upcoming production of Franz Werfel's book, *Song of Bernadette.*

She had never heard of the little French saint who had been canonized in 1933, but she was given a copy of the best-seller to read on the train, and by the time she reached California, was convinced that no one could portray Bernadette Soubirous better than she. Bernadette was a poor, sickly peasant girl who lived in Lourdes, France. In 1858, while still in her teens, she claimed to have seen the Virgin Mary in a grotto near the village. Her incredible tale divided the town in half, some believing, some criticizing, and she became one of the most controversial figures of her day. She eventually took the veil and later died of a bone disease, but never lost faith in the "beautiful lady" who told her she would not find happiness in this life, only the next.

Jennifer Jones was not the only actress interested in the role; nearly 2,000 applicants are said to have been tested and/or considered, but this was to be Fox's most prestigious film of the year, and to play the saintly part, they wanted an actress who was not known by the public and one whose life had not been touched by scandal. An actress fitting that description was not easy to find, and the list of possible Bernadette's grew smaller and smaller, with Anne Baxter, Linda Darnell and Mary Anderson being the most favorably considered.

Jennifer was tested soon after she arrived on the coast by Henry King, who had been signed to direct the costly film. The scene selected was when Bernadette sees "the lady" for the first time. A stick was held above the camera and she was told to imagine she was a 14-year-old peasant girl beholding a vision of the Blessed Virgin.

The same scene had been used to test the other candidates and, as King would later say, "I asked my editor to add [Jennifer's] scene on the reel with the others, so we could project them all together, and when we saw them all together, I noticed one outstanding thing. All of the others looked -- Jennifer actually saw." (See source no. B030.)

He contacted the studio's general manager, and within ten minutes Jennifer Jones was signed to play Bernadette. Fox wanted to own half of Jennifer's contract, but Selznick refused. Negotiations continued until Selznick finally agreed to a deal commiting Jennifer to making five films at Fox, one a year, for the next five years.

On December 9, 1942, the press announced that Jennifer Jones, an unknown actress under contract to David O. Selznick, had won the most coveted role of the year. Robert Walker, back in New York with a successful radio career, hardly had time to recover from the shock of his wife's sudden fame, when he himself was invited to test for a role in a Robert Taylor film at MGM. He easily won the scene-stealing part of the young soldier in *Bataan*, and it is is fairly certain that Selznick had a part in his being signed. Knowing

Robert Walker and Jennifer Jones, circa 1943. Courtesy of the Museum of Modern Art/Film Stills Archives.

that being separated from her husband was depressing Jennifer, and not wanting *anything* to affect her performance, he used his influence at MGM (L.B. Mayer was his father-in-law) and Robert Walker was suddenly a film actor. It was simple, but it made sense, and the reunited Walkers rented a small house in Beverly Hills and began adjusting to their new fairy tale life.

As Jennifer tackled George Seaton's 329-page script and learned camera technique by testing with the candidates for other roles, the Fox publicity department was generating reams of publicity about the young star, making her appear almost as saintly as Bernadette herself. It was strictly forbidden to mention her marriage or her children, and she was advised by Selznick to keep a low profile, to live a cloistered life, and for the sake of Bernadette, not to talk to the press about her husband and children!

By the time filming began on *Song of Bernadette* in March, 1943, Walker had completed his role in *Bataan*, another supporting part in *Madame Curie*, and had been cast as the lead in *See Here, Private Hargrove*. The word was also out -- he was married to Jennifer Jones and they were the parents of two children. Studio bosses were worried that the public would reject a Bernadette who was married, and a mother, but tried to counteract that possibility by filling the fan magazines with stories about the "happy, young, Cinderella couple, enjoying love and luck." It worked. The public fell in love with the handsome couple and their tow-headed boys, taking Walker to their collective hearts as the clumsy but good-natured Private Hargrove, and eagerly awaiting Jennifer's Bernadette.

Under Henry King's direction, the film was in production most of the summer. And King's cast was excellent, from Anne Revere as Bernadette's stern mother to Vincent Price as a village prosecutor. Playing a village priest was stage and film veteran Charles Bickford, who took Jennifer under his wing and taught her a great deal about film acting. They formed a close friendship that lasted until his death twenty-four years later.

As *Song of Bernadette* neared completion at Fox and Robert Walker filmed his last scenes as Private Hargrove at MGM, Selznick was busily preparing his next film venture. Based on a book by Dayton, Ohio, housewife Margaret Buell Wilder, in which she writes letters to her husband fighting in the war overseas, telling him about the war's effect on the American home, her home in particular, Selznick hoped *Since You Went Away* would rival *Gone With the Wind* in critical and public acclaim. Selznick wrote the screenplay himself, tailoring roles for Joseph Cotten, Agnes Moorehead, Shirley Temple and Monty Woolley. Claudette Colbert agreed to star as Anne Hilton, the wife and mother, and Selznick never considered anyone other than Jennifer for the role of Jane, the eldest daughter in the first bloom of womanhood.

The role was drastically different from Bernadette -- and a supporting one at that -- but Selznick insisted that Jennifer take it, explaining that he didn't want the public to identify her as a "sort of Bernadette in real life, an eminently worthy character, but lacking variety." (See source no. B023.) In the book, Jane had been a minor character, but Selznick enlarged it to being second in importance to Colbert's.

In an often-analyzed decision, Selznick cast Robert Walker as Corporal Bill Smollett, Jane's boyfriend, who is tragically killed in battle before they can marry.  There are several theories regarding his being signed: that Jenifer suggested it; that Selznick did it to put an end to rumors that his interest in Jennifer was more than professional; and that Walker was simply an ideal choice (which he was).  Another much darker and disturbing theory is that Selznick was exerting his power over the couple or, more specifically, over Walker.  Selznick was almost certainly in love with Jennifer by this time -- John Houseman even went as far to say that they were "involved" as early as August, 1941. (See source no. B023) -- and it is also likely that they were having an affair.  Walker must have been aware of the situation, and by casting him as Jennifer's lover in the film, Selznick was, in a strange and perverse way, telling him that although he could make love to Jennifer in *front* of the camera, *away* from it, he had no hold on her whatsoever!  Whatever his reasons were, Selznick wanted no one else but Walker for the part. That is certain.  Soon after filming began, Walker was incapacitated for a month due to a motorcycle accident.  It threw the production staff into a panic as scenes not even ready to be filmed, scenes not involving Walker's character, had to be  quickly whipped into shape.  It would have been simpler and less costly to replace him, but Selznick refused.

John Cromwell, who directed the film for Selznick, told film historian Lawrence G. Quirk, that Selznick was obsessed with Jennifer at this stage. "She was half-repelled, half-attracted by him.  They say money is sexy, but power is sexier.  David was all power, and I guess that got to her." (See source no. B035.)  Something certainly got to her, because in October, 1943, one month after filming began on *Since You Went Away*, Jennifer Jones and Robert Walker separated.

It occurred on a day when Jennifer and a few other cast members had been called back to Fox for *Song of Bernadette* retakes.  Actress Anne Revere remembered, "Jennifer announced her separation from Bob one morning. That afternoon a very long, sable coat was delivered to her at the studio -- a gift from David Selznick." (See source no. B023.)

Neither Bob nor Jennifer would publicly discuss the reasons they decided to separate and, in fact, the announcement was buried deep in the *Los Angeles Times*.  Before the fact became well known, three major studios -- MGM (Walker's home base), 20th Century-Fox (about to release *Song of Bernadette*), and United Artists (slated to release *Since You Went Away*) -- urged the couple to mend their broken marriage, but it was apparently hopeless.  The studios wanted their films safely released and making money before the public learned of their separation, and their efforts might have been successful had not *Ladies Home Journal*  printed the story in their January 1944 issue. (See source no. B089.)  A staffer on the magazine had already written an article about the couple and their idyllic marriage, but since the marriage had turned out to be less than ideal, the article would be an embarrassment to the magazine.  A re-write was ordered, and the shocking news hit the stands in December.

As Bernadette Soubirous.

Hollywood was surprised and disappointed, but the couple remained separated and silent as to why. In interviews, Jennifer rarely mentioned Bob. In fact, she rarely talked at all, the writer usually having to paraphrase the star's statements and pad the story with prosaic descriptions of her furnishings, her clothes, her sons and her penchant for gardening. Bob seemed more relaxed during interviews and often mentioned Jennifer, but only to praise her acting ability, to predict her bright future and to insist that she was a wonderful mother. He did say (in an article entitled "Sunday Pop." see source no. B061) that he would like to live at home again, indicating that the separation was not his idea.

After the separation became known, Selznick tended to devote more and more attention to Jennifer. Feeling that his star was excessively shy and projected little color off the screen, he hired noted cover girl and beauty consultant Anita Colby to tutor her in the areas of dress, make-up and conversation. Colby also taught Jennifer how to look people in the eye instead of lowering her head or looking away. The two became close friends, and remained so for many years.

*Song of Bernadette* premiered at Los Angeles's Carthay Circle on December 27 (just in time to qualify for the 1943 academy awards) and attracted a great deal of press coverage, with scores of celebrities showing up in minks and sables to see this eagerly awaited film. Mary Pickford clung to the arm of husband Buddy Rogers, Hedy Lamarr and Irene Dunne smiled for photographers, and Dinah Shore and George Montgomery made their first public appearance as husband and wife. (See source no. B101.) Noticeably absent was the film's star, Jennifer Jones, who was said to be ill. Although her "illness" was more likely a severe case of shyness, it is possible her health was less than perfect. She was in the middle of filming *Since You Went Away* and director John Cromwell later said that she was constantly nervous and upset. (See source no. B035.) It is known that she would become so distraught during the love scenes with Walker that she would flee the set in tears and run to her dressing room. Selznick would often have to coax her to return and finish the scene.

*Bernadette* was hailed as a great success, with a great deal of that success attributed to the sensitive and sincere performance of Jennifer Jones. The critics all agreed she was excellent and when the academy award nominations were announced in January, Jennifer was nominated as best actress of 1943 along with Ingrid Bergman (*For Whom the Bell Tolls*), Joan Fontaine (*The Constant Nymph*), Jean Arthur (*The More the Merrier*) and Greer Garson (*Madame Curie*).

The last scene for *Since You Went Away* was filmed on February 9, 1944, and Jennifer had a few weeks to rest before her next assignment, although she did travel to Tulsa for the nationwide opening of *Song of Bernadette* on February 25, where she was given a tremendous welcome at the train station. She was back in Hollywood for the academy award presentation on March 2, which was also her 25th birthday.

Wearing a simple tailored outfit, she sat nervously with Ingrid Bergman as Greer Garson (1942's winner) announced the best actress of

1943. To no one's surprise, it was Jennifer Jones!  To win an Oscar for her first important film was a great honor, and although she expressed surprise and gratitude when accepting her statuette, she admitted years later that it had meant little to her, that she had expected it, but that to win one now "would mean so much." (See source no. B131.)

In addition to the Oscar presented Jennifer, *Song of Bernadette* won Oscars in three of the other eleven categories for which it had been nominated: cinematography, interior set design and musical score, making it the winningest film of the year.

On March 3, the day following the academy award presentations, Jennifer Jones initiated divorce proceedings against Robert Walker. Although they had been separated for five months, it was hoped they could still get back together, and the announcement caused a flood of negative publicity, most of it directed at Jennifer herself. Typical was Janet Bentley's open letter to the academy award winner, which appeared in the March issue of *Photoplay*. "What the real truth is, we don't purport to know," Miss Bentley wrote. "But we do know that you have been innocently involved in wounding more people than you can possibly guess by this decision to part. It may not be within your powers to change the course of things, but if it is, please read this and then think -- just a little longer." (See source no. B052.) Another fan  magazine writer said that not since the break-up of Mary Pickford and Douglas Fairbanks in 1929 had a Hollywood divorce caused so much unhappiness.

The only objective voice seemed to belong to respected columnist Adela Rogers St. Johns. Writing for the June issue of *Photoplay*, she exposed the hostility toward Jennifer as simply an unfair expectation that she be a real-life Bernadette. "She is a girl with a life of her own," Miss St. Johns wrote. "It would be unjust to expect an actress of our times to dedicate her life to the spirit of a girl who lived so long ago in France." (See source no. B110.)  The article is an interesting commentary on the fact that a star's off-screen life was expected to correspond to his/her on-screen image.

The studios need not have feared the public rejecting Jennifer as Bernadette. The film was doing record business at the box office, and when *Since You Went Away* was released in July, it  also made a lot of money, with Jennifer winning kudos for her performance as Jane Hilton.  As Bosley Crowther said in his review for *The New York Times*, "[She is] surpassingly sweet as a well-bred American daughter in the first bloom of womanhood and love." (See source no. B030.)

The "first bloom of love" was Bill Smollet, the young corporal whom she loves and loses to the perils of war.  Her scenes with Smollet (played by Robert Walker) were acted with a sensitivity and tenderness that made them the highlight of the film.  Their separation at the station, declaring their love as his train pulls out, is heartbreaking to watch, and knowing that the on-screen lovers were seeking an off-screen divorce gave the scene an added sense of pathos.

Wanting to take advantage of the star's popularity -- and their one-picture-a-year deal with Selznick -- Fox demanded that Jennifer report to work on April 24.  They had cast her in the title role in *Laura*, but, for whatever reason, Selznick would not allow her to  accept the part.  When she failed to show up on the appointed day, Fox  filed a $613,000 damage suit against her, but Selznick was able to appease them by promising Jennifer's services for another, mutually agreed upon project .

In retrospect, it seems that Selznick's ability to determine what was best for Jennifer was already a bit faulty.  The role went to Gene Tierney, the film was hailed as a classic and it made Miss Tierney one of the most important film stars of the 40s.  The plot -- a beautiful and ambitious young woman becomes the object of an older man's obsession -- paralleled the Jones/Selznick relationship, and that is perhaps the reason Selznick didn't want his star associated with the project.  It couldn't have been because he had something else in mind for her; he had given *Spellbound* to Ingrid Bergman, and although he did buy the screenrights to Robert Nathan's fantasy novel, *Portrait of Jennie*, it was put aside for the future.  He did briefly consider remaking *Little Women*, with Jennifer as Jo.  Wardrobe tests were made and some footage was allegedly shot, but he soon lost interest and sold the project to MGM which made the film in 1949 with June Allyson.

Jennifer Jones was considered "hot property" and other studios were eager to have her on loan-out, keeping Selznick busy reading scripts sent for his approval.  He approved none, preferring to hold onto Jennifer until he could star her in a project of his own, a project "just right" for her abilities.  One script did catch his eye.  RKO had the rights to *Duel in the Sun*, and Niven Busch had been hired to adapt his own novel. RKO wanted Jennifer as Pearl Chavez, a sexy half-breed who ignites feelings of love and lust from two brothers, one bad, one good.  John Wayne was already signed to play Lewt, the bad brother who dies in climatic shoot-out with Pearl.  Jennifer was their third choice (Teresa Wright declined due to pregancy and MGM's Hedy Lamarr was unavailable) and Selznick, who realized the part was perfect, but was annoyed that she had not been their first choice, turned down the offer.  Unable to find a suitable Pearl, RKO then cancelled their plans to film Busch's novel and Selznick, who had hoped that would happen, quickly bought the rights. He had grandiose plans for the story;  it would be spectacularly filmed in color, would have the greatest cast ever assembled, and would be to the west what *Gone With The Wind* had been to the south. Pearl Chavez would be as memorable a heroine as Scarlet O'Hara.

He did realize that it would take some time to get his western epic ready for the cameras, and not wanting his most valuable star idle, he loaned her to Paramount for the bizarre *Love Letters*.  As Singleton, she falls in love with a man who she believes has been sending her beautiful love letters, although they were actually written by someone else.  She marries the bogus letter writer only to be abused and cruelly beaten.  Her foster mother (Gladys Cooper) kills the man, then suffers a stroke which renders her speechless and unable to defend Jennifer when it is *she* who is accused of the crime and sentenced to prison.  Despite a happy ending, the film was rather bleak and when released late in 1945, found little suport from critics although the public paid to see it and the Motion Picture Academy saw fit to nominate

Jennifer as best actress of that year, her third consecutive nomination (she lost to Joan Crawford).

In January, 1945, she was still busily filming *Love Letters* when the 1944 academy award nominations were announced, and for her performance as Jane Hilton in *Since You Went Away*, she was nominated as best supporting actress. Ethel Barrymore, returning to films after a 12-year hiatus, won the Oscar, but Jennifer did have the stage briefly when she presented to her friend, Ingrid Bergman, the Oscar for best actress of the year.

The Oscars were presented on March 15, 1945, two weeks after filming had finally begun on Selznick's massive *Duel in the Sun*, a film he believed would be his best to date. He made good his goal to film the lusty tale in glowing technicolor and to assemble a great cast. It may not have been the greatest ever, but it was certainly impressive, and included Herbert Marshall, Charles Bickford, Lionel Barrymore, Lillian Gish and Harry Carey. Jennifer was, of course, cast as the fiery Pearl and Gregory Peck and Joseph Cotten played the good and bad brothers respectively. Despite these assets, the film did not live up to Selznick's inflated expectations; it may have equalled *Gone With the Wind* in sheer spectacle, but not in greatness.

The film did not open until December 31, 1946, and critics were not kind, although they did wax enthusiastic over Jennifer's performance, even predicting that she would win the academy award. She didn't (losing to Olivia de Havilland), and some critics now say that she didn't even deserve the nomination, attributing it to Selznick's lobbying. The academy award debate aside, Jennifer *is* truly great in the role. Film historian Ken Wlaschin considers Pearl Chavez to be Jennifer's "greatest achievement -- there have been few more searingly carnal personifications of sexuality on the screen." (See source no. B045.) Pearl's voluptuousness, scant costuming and unbridled passion earned the film the nickname "lust in the dust," aroused censorial dismay and led the Catholic Church to forbid their members to see it, although everyone else must have. It was held over at almost every theatre at which it played and still ranks as one of the all-time box office champions.

Its budget estimated at the then-record sum of $7 million, *Duel in the Sun* was in production throughout the summer of 1945 in the hot Arizona desert and later at Lasky Mesa, just west of the San Fernando Valley. King Vidor, who received direction credit, actually walked off the picture before it was comepleted, fed up with Selznick's demanding memos and constant interference. He was replaced by William Dieterle, whose contribution was not noted.

Many years later, shortly before his death, King Vidor was interviewed for an oral history series sponsored by the Director's Guild. His memories of *Duel in the Sun* were vivid, and when asked about Selznick and his relationship with Jones, he said, "Selznick was madly in love with her. Everything he did was for her benefit. If the cameramen didn't make her look good in a close-up, they would have to go back and do it over again. He definitely had an obsession. He would breathe hard when he watched her scenes and when they were being shot."

About Jones, Vidor remembered, "She was one of those actresses who would really show what they were feeling in their facial expressions. I don't know if you could call them actresses, but they were certainly a photogenic lot. I enjoyed working with them. Their inner feelings show up very well."

He said Jennifer was told each day which scenes would be filmed, and how Pearl would be feeling inside, a chore some directors would object to.

"I didn't mind," Vidor said. "I thought she had a special quality. It's hard to express what she had in words, but a lot of silent film actors and actresses had it." (See source no. B009.)

He did say that he thought he could handle this "special quality" better than any other director for whom Jones worked, that he better understood how she had to first *feel* what the character was feeling. When she tried to *act* the feeling, it didn't work, he explained, and she resorted to facial grimaces.

Filming on *Duel* was completed in November and Jennifer started work almost immediately in *Cluny Brown* at Fox. Selznick feared that she hadn't had ample time to recover from the strain of playing Pearl, but she seemed to adapt beautifully to the direction of the almost legendary Ernst Lubitsch. Her leading man was Charles Boyer and the two seemed to have a great time in this "delectable and sprightly lampoon," as the film was called by *The New York Times*. (See source no. B030.) The critics were surprised by her comic abilities and complimented her perfect timing. It is a pity that Selznick did not allow her to develop this talent, preferring instead to confine her to heavy romantic drama.

With the release of *Cluny Brown* in June, and *Duel* in December, 1946 was a good film year for Jennifer Jones, and her accomplishments were recognized by *Look* magazine who presented her with their prestigious Achievement Award. It would be the last such year she would experience for almost a decade.

As soon as *Duel in the Sun* was ready for release, Selznick plunged into his next project -- *The Paradine Case*, with Gregory Peck and Alida Valli -- and Jennifer, inactive since the completion of *Cluny Brown*, spent the last half of 1946 wondering what her next film would be. Selznick was too involved in the new film to give her much attention, and she kept to herself, was rarely seen in public, avoided parties and her name was seldom mentioned in the press. She did dine occasionally with the Joseph Cottens, who had become close friends. Joe had been Jennifer's leading man in three films, and she hoped they could work together again.

That wish came true when, in early 1947, with Selznick again able to devote attention to Jennifer, he reunited them in *Portrait of Jennie*, Robert Nathan's gentle story of a painter named Eben Adams and his chance encounter with a strange little girl in Central park. Adams is a starving artist during the Depression who has become bitter and disillusioned, until he meets Jennie, a little girl who talks of things that happened long ago. She disappears into the misty night, but has inspired him to resume his painting. He encounters her on several other occasions, usually a week or so apart, but each time he sees her, she appears to have grown older, matured, and he finds himself falling in love, attracted to her ethereal beauty which he tries to

Charles Boyer and Jennifer Jones in a publicity portrait for *Cluny Brown* (1946). Courtesy of the Billy Rose Theatre Collection, New York Public Library at Lincoln Center, Astor, Lenox, and Tilden Foundations.

capture on canvas.  Although he soon loses her to the ghostly world from which she had come, his "Portrait of Jennie" remains, a tangible link to a timeless love.

Jennifer was perfectly cast as the fey ghost and Joseph Cotten was a natural as Adams.  In support, Selznick surrounded them with the likes of Ethel Barrymore, Cecil Kellaway, Lillian Gish and Florence Bates, and he sent the entire cast to New York in February to start location work, but halted the project after only two weeks of filming; he was dissatisfied with the script, the cost, the location sites and the way Jennifer photographed.  He hired a new writer and the cast waited for five weeks while the screenplay was revised.

Shooting resumed in April with Selznick on hand to see that the production went according to plan, and the plan was for filming to continue throughout the summer, both in New York and around Boston Harbor.  While David and Jennifer were in the East working on *Portrait*, the gossip columnists in the west, who had been hinting of a romance between the two for some time, suddenly began predicting a marriage.  Jennifer had been divorced from Robert Walker since 1945, but David and Irene Selznick were merely separated, and although David and Jennifer made no effort to conceal their romance, neither would comment on marriage.

Filming on *Portrait of Jennie* was finally completed in November, after several stops and starts, but Selznick wasn't entirely confident in the fragile story's ability to attract an audience.  He scrapped some footage, filmed additional scenes, added a pretentious prologue (narrated by Ben Hecht), expanded the storm climax to a sepia-toned, wide-screened hurricane, and succeeded only in holding up the film's release for another year.  The special effects won an Oscar, but they were out of place, throwing the delicate film dangerously off balance.

By the time *Portrait* premiered -- in March, 1949 -- The Selznicks had finally divorced, and Jennifer had appeared in a play at the La Jolla Playhouse and completed two films -- *We Were Strangers* for director John Huston, and *Madame Bovary* at MGM for director Vincente Minelli. *Portrait of Jennie*, over which Selznick had labored so long, was a box office flop of the first order, and the other two films also did poorly at the box office.  It was a devastating year professionally for both Jennifer and Selznick, and, sadly, it marked the end of the glory days for both of them.

(It's interesting to note that despite Jennifer's slippage in the American film market, she continued to be recognized abroad.  For her performance as *Madame Bovary*, she was selected as Best Foreign Actress of the year [1949] at the Paris Film Festival, and was awarded the the Film Francais Grand Prix des Directeurs de Cinema by the theatre managers of France and North Africa. See sources A10, A11.)

Regardless of the professional setbacks, 1949 was also a happy year.  If the gossip columns are correct, David Selznick had long intended to make Jennifer Jones his wife, and having been legally free from wife, Irene, since January, 1948, it was only Jennifer's reluctance that kept the two from tying the knot.  She reportedly didn't think marriage would be the best thing, but changed her mind while vacationing in Europe with Selznick that summer. On July 13, 1949, at the unusual hour of 8:30 a.m., Jennifer Jones (age thirty) and David O. Selznick (age forty-seven) became man and wife. The ceremony was performed in the middle of the Mediterranean Sea aboard a yacht called Manona, and was witnessed by the Leland Haywards and the Louis Jourdans. Later that day, to insure the legality of the marriage, their vows were spoken anew at the Genoa city hall.

After a week-long honeymoon aboard the Manona, the newlyweds arrived in London where Selznick's interest was peaked by Mary Webb's novel, *Gone to Earth*. He thought it would be a perfect vehicle for his wife and with his usual panache, began planning the film. Selznick did not involve himself in the actual production of the film, which was written, produced and directed by Michael Powell and Emeric Pressburger, the talented English team responsible for such classics as *Black Narcissus, The Life and Death of Colonel Blimp* and *The Red Shoes*. Set to be filmed on location and in color, Selznick hoped *Gone to Earth* would equal Powell and Pressburger's other successes. Sadly, it didn't.

Hazel Woodus, a superstitious gypsy who roams the hills of Shropshire, with lame animals as her companions, provided Jennifer with one of the most off-beat roles of her career, and although the color photography was lovely, and the English supporting cast, including David Farrar and Cyril Cusack, a strong one, the film was not a success when released in England. Jennifer's acting did not come under fire, but her accent did, many critics calling it phoney, a criticism director Powell considers unfair.

"I thought her accent was fine," he later told film editor Karen Latham Everson. "My mother was from that area of England and I was very familiar with that particular accent." Powell said that on the set, Jones was "professional, but not coldly professional. She would often chat with the crew, and I sensed that she would have enjoyed talking to them even more, had not Selznick occupied so much of her time." (See endnote.)

Although Selznick did not produce the film, he did own the North American distribution rights, and when he and Jennifer returned to California early in 1951, he set about to "improve" the film before releasing it to American theatres. What he eventually did was import most of the English cast to California, re-shoot several scenes under the direction of Rouben Mamoulian, excise other scenes, and change the title. This prevented American audiences from seeing it until 1952 when it was released as *The Wild Heart,* but Selznick's efforts were wasted; the public was indifferent and the film quickly disappeared from theatre marquees.

While Selznick was still trying to salvage *Gone to Earth*, Jennifer started working at Paramount in *Carrie*. Based on Theodore Dreiser's *Sister Carrie*, it was directed by William Wyler and contained one of Laurence Olivier's strongest film performances, and although Wyler thought Jones fine in the title role, critics did not generally agree. Shelved for over a year while Paramount executives debated over how to market the film, it was finally released in June, 1952, shortly after *The Wild Heart*, but it was during the McCarthy Era, and the film's Communistic overtones and downbeat attitude, prevented it from becoming popular. In fact, it was a box office disaster.

*Carrie*'s production had begun early in the summer of 1950, and, shortly afterwards, Louella Parsons hinted in her column that Jennifer was pregnant. Jennifer denied the rumor, but Louella had been right. She was aware of her pregnancy before filming on *Carrie* began, and when Wyler asked why she had not mentioned it, she said she had feared it would have cost her the part. Her role was an especially difficult one, and there was often tension on the set between Wyler and Selznick. Selznick had no part in the film's production, but was constantly giving unsolicited advice to Wyler as to how the film should be directed. Wyler ignored Selznick's advice and finally told him -- nicely but firmly -- not to visit the set. Added to this frustration for Jennifer were the heavy period costumes. Despite Wyler's offer to film her mostly in close-up, avoiding full-figure shots, Jennifer insisted on binding her waist with tight corsets every day to achieve the small waistline required by the role. In Axel Madsen's *William Wyler*, the director recalls that "just watching her made me uncomfortable. She lost the baby after the picture. How much the strapping of her waist had to do with it I don't know." (See source no. B027.)

Jennifer's scenes were completed in November, and on December 16, 1950, she suffered a miscarriage. It was a major disappointment for the Selznicks. David had two sons from his previous marriage, and Jennifer had two sons by Robert Walker, and they had hoped their child would be a daughter.

*Carrie* was Jennifer's fifth straight failure, and to regain her foothold in a community where "you're only as good as your last picture" was just as true as ever, she desperately needed a hit. Not quite the blockbuster she needed, but close enough to it, was *Ruby Gentry*, which premiered late in 1952. Before the film was released, in fact, long before it was even in production, Jennifer took a hiatus from filmwork. Weary from working in two films back to back and depressed after losing her baby, she traveled to South Korea in 1951 to visit wounded soldiers near the front line. For this unselfish and unpublicized mission, she received a special citation from the American Red Cross and a gold medal from General Van Fleet, field commander of the United Nations Forces.

Selznick later joined her, and they were still vacationing in Europe when, on August 29, 1951, Robert Walker died in his Hollywood apartment at the age of 33. Since his 1945 divorce from Jennifer, he had suffered a series of nervous breakdowns and had been arrested on several drunk and disorderly charges. Minutes before his death, he had been injected with sodium amytal to calm another of his emotional outbursts.

Jennifer immediately flew back to California to be with her sons. She didn't allow them to attend his funeral in Utah, wanting them to remember their father "as he was." (See source no. B023).

She took the boys to Europe in September. They were enrolled in a Swiss school, and little was heard from the Selznicks until May, 1952, when

As Pearl Chavez.

Gregory Peck and Jennifer Jones in *Duel in the Sun* (1946).

Jennifer was signed to play *Ruby Gentry*, a woman who, so the ads proclaimed, wrecked a town man by man and sin by sin.

Regarded as King Vidor's last important film, *Ruby Gentry* gave Jennifer Jones one of her best roles and her biggest hit since 1946. Not since *Duel in the Sun* had her films made money, and *Ruby Gentry* proved that with the right script and right direction (Vidor also directed her in *Duel*), she could still be popular with the public. And in this melodramatic tale of a girl from the wrong side of the tracks who takes revenge on her boyfriend for marrying a "more respectable" woman, the public loved her. *The Los Angeles Times* predicted the film would attract a lot of attention because "of the presence of Jennifer Jones, whose excellence as a film actress cannot be questioned." (See source no. B030.) Also attracting attention were the love scenes between Jones and rugged Charlton Heston. Torrid and sensual, their scenes together rivalled those between Jones and Gregory Peck in *Duel* as some of the steamiest ever put on film.

No doubt bitterly recalling the unhappy experience of working under Selznick's thumb on *Duel in the Sun*, Vidor succeeded in filming *Ruby Gentry* with no interference from the star's husband, although Selznick did have a hand in the film's editing.

If Jennifer had folowed *Ruby Gentry* with another success, her faltering career might have been strengthened and she could have charged into the 50's as a major star. But it didn't happen that way.

Impressed by Italian director Vittorio De Sica's neorealist style, Selznick approached him with an offer to direct a film starring Jennifer Jones. After prolonged negotiations, both agreed the film would be *Terminal Station*, the story of an American housewife on the last night of her vacation in Rome, having a last-minute tryst with her lover before her train leaves. Montgomery Clift was signed to play the Italian lover.

The film went into production in Rome, during December, 1952, with Selznick producing and De Sica directing. The two clashed from the beginning, De Sica preferring a spontaneous, improvised method of filming and Selznick insisting that a shooting script be followed. Several writers (including Truman Capote) contributed to the script, but what evolved after a long and troubled production, was a film totally unworthy of the talent that had gone into its making. It ran for nearly two hours when released in Europe, and although the reviews were respectable, Selznick refused to release the film in America without a re-edit; he cut the film down to a mere 63 minutes, removing practically every scene that did not include Jones and Clift, and released it to American theatres during the summer of 1954 as *Indiscretion of an American Wife*. The film failed miserably, although Jennifer was complimented by critics for looking so lovely in the tight close-ups, of which there were literally dozens.

Following the ill-fated experience with De Sica, after Selznick had taken the film to America for extensive editing, Jennifer opted to remain in Italy during the summer of 1953, where she was approached by director John Huston; he and Humphrey Bogart were planning to make a film in Italy and wanted her for one of the leads. She accepted.

*Beat the Devil* seems to have been a spontaneous venture from the onset, with no one exactly sure what was happening. It was not a success when released in the states early in 1954, but has acquired a cult following over the years. As critics have since pointed out, *Beat the Devil* is a clever film when viewed closely, a sort of parody of Huston's own style, of Bogart's persona and of tall tales in general. The feeling of spontaneity is undoubtedly due to the screenplay being written (mostly by Truman Capote) only hours ahead of each day's filming.

Most of the film's action takes place in a small Italian seaport where a motley group is waiting for a ship captain to sober up enough to take them to Africa. The group includes middle-aged roustabout Bogart, his Anglophile Italian wife, Gina Lollobrigida, his bizarre business associates, Peter Lorre and Robert Morley, and an English couple, pompous Edward Underdown and his compulsive liar wife, Jennifer Jones (in a blonde wig). They are all invloved in a vague scheme to get their hands on a piece of uranium-rich land in East Africa.

*Beat the Devil* was Jennifer's second and last comedy, but its black humor was not appreciated at the time. The film's failure, coupled with the abysmal reception of *Indiscretion* shortly after, made 1954 one of the bleakest years of Jennifer Jones's career, and caused her to question her own ability. She retreated to the Beverly Hills mansion on Tower Road that once belonged to actor John Gilbert where Selznick threw large, ornate parties and she usually stayed in her room. Although she was glamorous Mrs. Selznick on the outside, she was still Phylis Isley on the inside, a pretty, dark-haired girl from Oklahoma who was so shy she couldn't look people in the eye. She was a woman of contrasts, and a woman on whom there was a great deal of pressure to succeed. Selznick had invested a great deal of money in her career, starring her in several highly expensive productions, but most of these films had failed, slowly destroying his once-solid reputation and depleting his bank account. 1954 was indeed a year of failure, and Jennifer must have blamed herself.

The year wasn't a total loss, however;  after David and Jennifer returned from Italy in January, Paramount offered her the title role in their upcoming production of *The Country Girl*, opposite Bing Crosby and William Holden. She signed the contract and had already posed for advance publicity pictures when she suddenly withdrew from the project. She was pregnant and decided her health was more important than a film role. Grace Kelly took over and won an Oscar for her performance.

On August 12, 1954, Jennifer gave birth to a seven-pound, eight-ounce girl. She was named Mary Jennifer, and was the daughter both had wanted for so long. She was the only child the couple would have.

Despite the joy of motherhood, Jennifer's bad professional luck showed no sign of easing. Disappointed with her recent filmwork, she decided the stage would be a good change of pace, and on December 21, 1954, Jennifer Jones made her Broadway debut at the newly-refurbished ANTA Theatre in *Portrait of a Lady*. Based on the novel by Henry James, the play was adapted by William Archibald, directed by Jose Quintero and with sets by William and Jean Eckart, gowns by Cecil Beaton and a cast that included Cathleen Nesbitt, Eric Fleming and Barbara O'Neil, it should have been a hit. It wasn't, and the critics blamed the script, which they found woefully weak. The play closed after seven performances and Jennifer, whose interpretation of Isabel Archer had also been criticized, was bitterly disappointed. "I was bleeding from every pore," she later admitted. "I wanted to run to Tahiti and hide." (See source no. B023.)

She returned to California, depressed and unsure of herself, hoping the streak of bad luck would end. And then, suddenly, it did. 20th Century-Fox, for whom she had starred as Bernadette, offered her a three picture deal. It isn't entirely clear whether Selznick was responsible for the offer through industry manipulation or if the studio bosses simply considered her a worthy investment. Whatever the reason, the deal was quickly negotiated, the contract signed, and Jennifer was almost immediately given her first assignment which would prove to be the most successful.

Directed by Henry King (who had directed *Song of Bernadette*) and filmed on location in Hong Kong, using natural color and CinemaScope, *Love is a Many-Splendored Thing* was phenomenally successful, launched a hit song and re-established Jones as an actress of quality. It was based on the life of Dr. Han Suyin, and in the film, Jennifer (as the Eurasian Dr. Suyin), falls in love with war correspondent William Holden and fights prejudice at the hospital where she works. She loses both her fight and her lover at the film's end, and the unabashed sentiment, reminiscent of films from the 1930s, annoyed some critics but pleased the dewy-eyed public, who voted Jones their favorite actress of the year.

For the fifth and last time to date, she was nominated as best actress by the Motion Picture Academy, but the Oscar went to the fiery Italian actress Anna Magnani. The film was also nominated, but *Marty* was the year's surprise winner.

Jones and William Holden were handsome screen lovers; the chemistry between them was just right, but the off-screen chemistry between them went sour. In *Golden Boy, the Untold Story of William Holden*, Bob Thomas says that Jones was often irritated by Holden and complained about him to Selznick. Holden apparently attempted to call a truce by presenting his leading lady with a bouquet of white roses. She responded by throwing them back in his face. (See source no. B041.)

Her next film at Fox was the equally sentimental but much more gentle *Good Morning, Miss Dove*, in which she aged some 30 years, from a young, unhappy woman who had no choice but to become a school teacher, to a bitter, middle aged spinster, still a teacher, who is about to undergo a serious operation. Told via flashback, Miss Dove learns that in her three decades of teaching, she has inspired many people, and that she is much loved by her students, both past and present. Her heartwarming performance was a fine character study, highly praised by critics, but the film rarely surfaces.

Her final film of the Fox agreement was the weakest of the three. Gregory Peck had the title role in *The Man in the Gray Flannel Suit*, and as his wife, Jennifer's role was secondary and she resorted to neurotic

At the height of melodrama—with Charlton Heston in *Ruby Gentry* (1952). Courtesy of the Billy Rose Theatre Collection, New York Public Library at Lincoln Center, Astor, Lenox, and Tilden Foundations.

In costume for *Portrait of a Lady* (1954). Courtesy of the Billy Rose Theatre Collection, New York Public Library at Lincoln Center, Astor, Lenox, and Tilden Foundations.

mannerisms that critics were quick to point out. The film was released in the spring of 1956, and by that time, Jennifer was negotiating a particularly exciting deal with MGM -- to star in the remake of their 1934 Norma Shearer vehicle, *The Barretts of Wimpole Street.*

It had been her life-long dream to portray Elizabeth Barrett Browning, and nearly 20 years after she and Robert Walker, as young, starry-eyed academy students, had enacted a scene from the romantic play as their audition, she was finally getting her chance to play the famous poetess. The contract was quickly signed and filming began on location in London, with Sidney Franklin directing.

Franklin had also directed the 1934 version, and when the remake was released early in 1957, it was obvious that his skill had kept pace with the improvements in film technique over the last 23 years. Utilizing MetroColor, CinemaScope, authentic locations and costumes and a first rate cast headed by the formidable Sir John Gielgud, critics agreed the film was superior to the earlier version, some venturing to say that Jennifer's performance was better than Shearer's had been.

In February, 1957, as *The Barretts of Wimpole Street* was opening to critical acclaim, production was beginning in Italy's Alpine resort area on a film that would bring unhappiness to all concerned. So catastrophic was the failure of *A Farewell to Arms*, that it ended Selznick's career as a producer and took Jennifer off the screen for three years. She has made only four films since.

Twentieth Century-Fox, for which Jones had worked so successfully in the past, agreed to finance and distribute the film. Selznick was still trying to make a film that would eclipse *Gone With the Wind*, and he thought this would be the one. He was sure that "Catherine Barkley" would do for Jennifer Jones what "Scarlet O'Hara" had done for Vivien Leigh. He should have known that lightning doesn't strike twice.

John Huston was signed to direct Ben Hecht's screenplay and Rock Hudson was borrowed from Universal to play the American ambulance driver who falls in love with war nurse Jones. Hemingway's novel concentrates not on the love affair, but on the evils of war, and Huston wanted to remain loyal to the novel, but Seznick disagreed. He wanted the film to focus on the love affair, especially his wife, and insisted that the war be treated as a sub-plot. Both headstrong and stubborn, Huston and Selznick could not reach an agreement, and barely a month after filming began, Huston resigned in an outburst of emotional temperament.

In his autobiography, *An Open Book*, Huston discusses his disagreements with Selznick, blaming them on the deterioration of Selznick's once-sound judgment, and he attributes that deterioration to the man's obsession with Jennifer Jones.

"His love for her was real and touching," he says, "but in it lay the seeds of the failures that marked the last years of his life. Everything he did was for Jennifer, to the detriment of his own judgment... He didn't do anything worth a damn after he married Jennifer." (See source no. B016.)

(Huston didn't seem to feel any animosity toward Jennifer. Another book on the director reveals that he named a pet fox terrier Jenny in her honor. See source no. B017.)

The less temperamental Charles Vidor was quickly hired to replace Huston as director, and filming began anew. As the production wore on into the summer, stretching the proposed budget of time and money, worried Fox executives pressured Selznick to finish the film and rush it into release by Christmas. Selznick obliged, filming was completed in September, and he and Jennifer returned to California, anxious for the "masterpiece" to be unveiled.

Running 152 minutes, *A Farewell to Arms* premiered on December 18, 1958, at Grauman's Chinese Theatre in Los Angeles. It had been long and eagerly awaited, but the expected praise turned to merciless criticism. Selznick was severely berated for mutilating Hemingway's fondly-remembered love story, with critics being especially put off by the shockingly detailed and agonizing birth of the still-born child, a scene which they labelled an "obstetrical orgy." Jennifer was not spared, although the criticism was not so much of her acting, but of her age. In the novel, Catherine was 24, and Jones, at 39, was just not capable of portraying the nurse's youthful innocence. Hollis Alpert, writing for *Saturday Review*, perhaps said it best: "Jennifer Jones has a great deal of skill as an actress, but she's a fairly mature woman now... and that big movie screen has a gruesome way of revealing the disparity between what might be termed screen age and actual age." (See source no. B030.)

Despite its critical failure, the film made money; in its first two weeks of general release, it took in $350,000, in Los Angeles alone, a then-impressive figure, but the critics had broken Selznick's spirit and he retired, never to make another film. It must have been especially painful to realize that he had fatally wounded the career of his wife, for whom he had such wonderful plans.

Jennifer once admitted that harsh criticism hurt her deeply and made her "want to run away and hide" (see souce no. B023), and *Farewell*'s failure sent her into seclusion. She rejected film offers, refused interviews and began studying yoga "not as a philosophy," she said later, "but as exercise." (See source no. B138.) She remained in this state of limbo for three years.

Selznick had long been interested in filming F. Scott Fitzgerald's 1934 novel *Tender is the Night*, but plans didn't materialize until he sold the rights to 20th Century-Fox. Jennifer Jones and Jason Robards were hired to star, and other pivotal roles were given to Jill St. John, Tom Ewell and Joan Fontaine. Location work began in May, 1961, in Zurich and later on the French Riviera, but Selznick remained in Hollywood, uninvolved, although he did speak to his wife nightly on the telephone advising her in her interpretation of Nicole Diver, a woman recovering from a nervous breakdown.

Hollywood veteran Henry King directed (he later said he had accepted the job *only* because Jennifer was in the cast) and the filming went smoothly and finished on schedule, in time for a release in February, 1962. Usually shunning publicity reviews, Jennifer told United Press reporter Joseph

Jennifer Jones, circa 1952. Courtesy of the Billy Rose Theatre Collection, New York Public Library at Lincoln Center, Astor, Lenox, and Tilden Foundations.

Finnigan that for her role she had tested a "new approach" to acting. "A great deal of my new way... is personal,"she said."I do feel I've found a new world." She said that when the film opened she would watch with interest, trying to see "one moment of thought on that screen. I feel this picture will be a turning point in my career." (See source no. B138.)

Her "new approach" wasn't appreciated by critics, unfortunately. The 146-minute film was panned and Jones was not particularly well liked, although several reviewers commented that she had been perfectly cast as a neurotic, her nervous grimaces seeming natural to the emotionally disturbed Nicole. It *could* be considered a turning point of sorts; it was her last film of quality for over a decade, and despite the brief flurry of interest in her, Hollywood had nothing else to offer. She and David spent the better part of the next two years abroad.

In December, 1964, during one of their trips back to California, Selznick was sent the script of *Goddess on the Couch*, a funny play about a psychiatrist's wife. Both felt it would be a perfect vehicle for Jennifer's return to Broadway, and scheduled a trial run the following spring in Palm Beach and Miami, Florida. Retitled *The Man With the Perfect Wife*, the play opened in late April and amused Florida tourists, but critics found the third act weak. Not wanting his sensitive wife to face another possible Broadway failure, Selznick cancelled his plans to bring the play to New York later in the year.

David didn't remain in Florida for the run of the play, but went to New York where he suffered a series of heart attacks. He was back in California by the time Jennifer returned in late April, but not having been told of the attacks, she was shocked by his failing health and devoted herself to making his life stress-free. On June 23, 1965, for the first time in weeks, Selznick left his home to keep a lawyer's appointment in Beverly Hills. In the middle of the meeting, he began having chest pains and an ambulance rushed him to Mount Sinai hospital at 1 p.m. Jennifer arrived twenty minutes later and watched through a glass partition as doctors tried valiantly to save his life. An hour later, at 2:33 p.m., at age sixty-three, David O. Selznick died.

At a memorial service held at Forest Lawn Cemetery on June 25, Katharine Hepburn, Cary Grant and Joseph Cotten were among those who eulogized the mighty producer. Pallbearers included William Wyler, Sam Spiegel, Christopher Isherwood, William Paley and Alfred Hitchcock. Jennifer was the sole beneficiary of his one-million-dollar life insurance policy.

Despite her wealth as Selznick's widow, Jennifer was lonely and bored and wanted to go back to work. Later in the year, when Kim Stanley became ill and withdrew from the English production of *The Idol*, Jennifer was offered the part and flew immediately to London to take over the role of a medical student's mother who is willingly seduced by her son's beatnik friend on New Year's Eve. The film was bizarre, Jennifer's acting not impressive and the film quickly disappeared after its release in August 1966. Another failure was not what her sagging self esteem needed and she grasped at another chance for success by accepting the role of Georgie Elgin in the New

York stage production of Clifford Odet's play *The Country Girl*. She had missed out on the 1954 film role, and was particularly anxious to star in the City Center Drama Company's production which was part of the American Playwrights Series. It was booked for a limited engagement (September 29 - October 16, 1966) and also starred Rip Torn and Joseph Anthony (who replaced an ill Franchot Tone).

Regardless of Jennifer's fondness of the role, her performance fell far short of critics' expectations. "Miss Jones read most of her lines in a dull, listless fashion and appeared to be unconscious of the fact that she was playing with other actors," said Chauncy Howell in *Women's Wear Daily*, and Vincent Canby, in his review for the *New York Times*, said her performance was "cruel when it should be vital and petulant when it should be angry." (See source no. B023).

Another failed try for acceptance was apparently more than she could stand, and she returned to her very private life, seldom being seen outside her large Beverly Hills home on Tower Road. Not a word was heard from or about her for over a year until, suddenly, on Thursday night, November 9, 1967, she was found unconscious at the base of a Mailbu cliff, the Pacific waves lapping at her body. Alerted by Jennifer's physican that the actress had phoned him from Malibu threatening suicide, the police spotted her deserted car at the top of the cliff, and followed her dainty footprints down the steep incline. It appeared that she had fallen nearly one hundred feet to where she was found. She had stopped breathing but her heart was still beating faintly, and after being treated at a local hospital, she was rushed to Mount Sinai where she lay unconscious for six hours.

The next day, a shocking photo of her being wheeled into the emergency room, a breathing tube inserted into her mouth, appeared on the front page of several big city newspapers. In a bold headline, New York's *Daily News* announced JENNIFER JONES FOUND IN SURF, and for the next several days, reported her condition. She was discharged on November 13, but no explanation for the suicide attempt was ever offered.

In their investigation, the Malibu police discovered that soon before Jennifer was found, she had checked into a nearby motel under the name Phylis Walker, an interesting detail that the actress would never publicly comment on. Is it possible that she was remembering (or longing for) the happiness she had known as Mrs. Robert Walker, before Hollywood, before David O. Selznick, before their lives had become hopelessly complicated? The answer may never be known.

She was out of the news for another year or so, but reached the absolute nadir of her career in 1969, when she starred in *Angel, Angel Down We Go*, an embarrassingly bad film involving ritual murder, drugs and perversion. Playing a former star of porn films, Jennifer perhaps fared better than other cast members, but the few critics who bothered to see it were shocked that the once beautiful and saintly Bernadette would utter such trashy lines as "I've made thirty stag films and never faked an orgasm." Few theatres would even book the film, and it disappeared almost as quickly as it

David O. Selznick and Jennifer Jones, circa 1954. Courtesy of the Billy Rose Theatre Collection, New York Public Library at Lincoln Center, Astor, Lenox, and Tilden Foundations.

had appeared.  It surfaced again in 1971 as *Cult of the Damned*, but soon vanished and is best forgotten.

Late in 1969, as *Angel, Angel Down We Go* was dying a quick and painless death, Jennifer became interested in the Los Angeles-based Manhattan Project, a program devoted to setting up Salvation Army-type residential treatment facilities for drug-addicted youths.  She volunteered weekly, often had groups of fifteen or more young drug addicts in her home on weekends and was instrumental in opening up a new facility near Salt Lake City, Utah.  Having found a worthy outlet for her nervous energies, she seemed happy and began to emerge from her self-built coccoon.  She was still shy, however, and seldom accepted invitations to dinners or parties.  One she *did* accept was to attend a lavish party at the California home of Walter Annenberg on May 5, 1971.

Among the guests was millionaire Norton Simon, an avid art collector who had become interested in obtaining the portrait of Jones that Selznick had commissioned for *Portrait of Jennie*.  He engaged her in conversation, and by the end of the party, had become as fond of the model as he was of the painting.  A conservative Republican who had lost a 1970 race for the California senate, he had recently divorced his wife of 37 years, and it was only natural that these two, lonely, middle-aged people should start spending time together.

Two weeks later they took a sudden trip to Paris, realized they were in love, and on May 30 -- twenty five days after having met -- they were married at four in the morning aboard a launch in the middle of the English Channel, with Dover's white cliffs barely in sight. Sixty-four-year-old Simon explained his whirlwind romance with fifty-two-year-old Jones as "soul communication. There was... great simpatico between us right from the start." According to Jennifer, "he walked me around Paris and London until I was so exhausted I couldn't resist him anymore." She said their impromptu wedding "was the most romantic thing that's ever happened to me." (See source no. B149.)

Jennifer moved into Simon's Malibu estate and began a new life. She spent most of her time hostessing parties for her husband's influential friends (a frequent guest was Henry Kissinger) and learning about art.  She admitted to an interviewer that museums had always bored her, but through her husband's eyes she had learned to appreciate fine paintings and could now discuss the Masters "with an expertise I [can't] believe [is] mine." (See source no. B167.)

As for her children, Robert Jr. had followed his parents' footsteps into the movies and Michael was also appearing in occasional film and televison roles. Mary Jennifer, not surprisingly, had also expressed an interest in acting and in 1973 began studying in New York with Uta Hagen.

Jennifer's interest in acting was still strong too, it seems.  Early in 1974, after Olivia de Havilland turned down the lonely widow role in Irwin Allen's disaster epic *The Towering Inferno*, it was offered to Jennifer, who surprisingly accepted.  With a budget of fourteen million dollars, the film revolved around the survivors and victims of a catastrophic fire in a 138-

story San Francisco skyscraper. The all-star cast included Paul Newman, William Holden, Faye Dunnaway, Steve McQueen, Richard Chamberlain and Fred Astaire who, as a fake bond salesman, woos Jennifer before the fire erupts.

*The Towering Inferno* was Jennifer's first quality production in thirteen years, and the role of Lisolette Mueller was a particularly demanding one, forcing her to crawl through the burnt-out wreckage of the building trying to save her life, only to plunge to her death from a suspended glass elevator.

On the arm of her husband, a beaming Jennifer attended the premier on December 10, 1974, and was pleased by the film's favorable reception. Her work was also received favorably, the *Hollywood Reporter* finding her "looking fit and attractive." They added, "she not only gets to play romantic scenes... but also struggles gamefully through tough physical ordeals." (See source no. B030.) Other critics were equally impressed and she was even nominated for a Golden Globe award as best supporting actress.

In the light of this triumph, it is likely that Jennifer would have accepted another film role had not personal tragedy struck. On May 11, 1976, Mary Jennifer Selznick jumped to her death from the roof of a 22-story hotel in Los Angeles. She was 21 years old.

Jennifer was devastated, and Simon attempted to take his wife's mind off the loss by naming her as chairman of directors of the Norton Simon Museum in Pasadena, with its collection of paintings valued in the hundreds of millions. She assumed her new role in September, 1977, and met the challenge admirably. She also became involved with the Huntington Disease Council, and in addition to her charity work, three beauty experts (Carrie White, Vidal Sassoon and George Masters), in January of the same year, deemed the 57-year-old former star the most beautiful woman in the world. Her only explanation for her youthful appearance was swimming daily, some yoga and occasional bicycling. (See source no. B134.) Despite the bitter loss of her daughter, Jennifer once again appeared happy, and the time seemed right for another film. It never happened.

For a while, it looked hopeful; an announcement was made that she and Paul Newman would star in *The Day the World Ended*, another Irwin Allen disaster film, but plans fell through, and although she purchased the film rights to Larry McMurtry's novel *Terms of Endearment*, she later sold them to Paramount (who filmed the story in 1983 with Shirley MacLaine). Simon also attempted to get his wife back into the movies by taking an option on *The Jean Harris Story,* the tragic tale of schoolteacher Harris who killed her lover, Dr. Herman Tarnower, the creator of the Scarsdale Diet, but the option was allowed to expire, and rumors of a Jennifer Jones comeback have not surfaced since.

Despite the dearth of filmwork, Jennifer has not lacked for things to do. She is often mentioned in society columns when attending big, glamorous parties, and she has continued to devote a good deal of energy to various charities (in 1980 she donated one million dollars to the fight against mental illness), and yet she still finds time for her duties at the Norton Simon

As the bizarre Astrid in *Angel, Angel, Down We Go* (1969).

Museum. In April 1980, she represented her husband at an auction at London's famed Southeby Gallery and bid the then-record sum of 3.74 million dollars for Dutch artist Dieric Bout's 15th Century rendition of the Resurrection of Christ.

When Simon was striken in early 1984 with Guillain-Barre syndrome, an inflamation of the muscle nerves that results in paralysis and sometimes death, Jennifer maintained a vigil at his bedside. Stirred by the reports of her steadfastness during her husband's agonizing illness, and partly because of her charitable contributions, the University of Pennsylvania's School of Nursing honored her in September 1985, for her efforts "to promote a fairer, more compassionate society." She looked especially fetching in a long, red dress as she stood to accept the honor and thanked the large audience for their attendance. (See source no. B147.)

In March 1989, the 82-year-old Simon announced that he had relinquished the presidency of his museum with its fabled art collection, to his wife. Some concern was voiced by local art authorities who feared the collection might be scattered, but Jennifer's qualifications and expertise were not questioned. "She's well schooled in what he [Simon] would like," said Henry Hopkins, director of the Frederick R. Weisman Art Foundation. "Probably nobody's better versed... as to what his wishes are." (See source no. B157.)

Jennifer's involvement with the museum has limited her recent show business activities to sporadic appearances on televised award shows. In 1984, she was on hand to congratulate Lillian Gish at the American Film Institute's tribute to the legendary actress with whom she had co-starred in *Duel in the Sun* and *Portrait of Jennie*, and she made a surprise appearance on the 1987 Academy Award ceremony. Looking lovely, but visibly nervous, she was introduced following a montage of her best film moments, but her voice trembled and her hands shook as she announced the winner of the best cinematography Oscar. Later at a party, she confessed to having had an attack of nerves.

She was back in the limelight again in March 1989, as part of the American Film Institute's tribute to Gregory Peck. Belying her 70 years, she seemed more relaxed than usual when she turned to Peck and, with a youthful smile, admitted that playing love scenes with him in *Duel in the Sun* "wasn't exactly the hardest job I've ever had to do." It was hard to believe that 43 years had passed since those sizzling scenes had caused such controversy.

It was also hard to believe that 50 years had passed since a young, dark-eyed girl from Oklahoma named Phylis Isley was first introduced to the movie-going public.

Endnote:
Karen Latham Everson and her husband, film historian William K. Everson, are close friends of the Michael Powells, and the quoted conversation took place at a dinner party in September, 1988, in New York City.

Jennifer Jones, circa 1942.

# 2
# *Chronology*

1919 **March 2**: Born Phylis Lee Isley in Tulsa, Oklahoma, to Philip R. and Flora Mae Suber Isley.

1925 **March 2**: On her sixth birthday, allegedly tells parents that she intends to be an actress when grown.

1932 **Autumn**: Enrolls at Monte Cassino Junior College in Tulsa, a private school of the Benedictine Sisters.

1936 **Spring**: Is voted May Queen of the senior class; graduates with honors.

**September**: Enters the freshman class of Northwestern University as a drama major.

**December**: Accompanies parents to New York during Christmas break and sees Katherine Cornell in *Wingless Victory* five times.

1937 **Summer**: Joins the Mansfield Players as leading lady during their summer tour of the southwest.

**Autumn**: Auditions before the admission judges of the American Academy of Dramatic Arts (AADA) in New York City on September 10; is accepted.

1938 **January 2**: Meets fellow AADA student Robert Walker.

**Summer**: Returns to Oklahoma to act in summer stock.

**Autumn**: She and Walker do not return to AADA but seek stage work; eventually find work at the Cherry Lane Theatre in Greenwich

Village.

1939 **January 2**: She and Walker marry in Tulsa, Oklahoma.

**June 25**: Signs a $75-a-week contract with Republic; assigned female lead in *New Frontier*, a minor John Wayne western.

**July**: Assigned the only female role in the 15-part serial, *Dick Tracy's G Men*.

**Autumn**: She and Walker return to New York to seek stage work.

1940 **April 15**: Robert Walker, Jr. born.

1941 **March 13**: Michael Ross Walker born.

**April**: Sees *Claudia* and auditions for Chicago opening; loses to Phyllis Thaxter.

**July 21**: Hearing that Selznick has bought the film rights to the play, she auditions for role to Katherine Brown, Selznick's New York representative.

**July 22**: Called back to read for David O. Selznick.

**July 26**: Signed to a 7-year film contract, starting at $200 per week.

**August**: Appears in *Hello, Out There* at the Lobrero Theatre in Santa Barbara, California.

1942 **January 24**: Receives official name "Jennifer Jones." Press introduces her as Selznick's newest discovery.

**October**: Tests for role of Bernadette for Fox in California.

**November**: MGM tests and signs Robert Walker; assigned supporting role in *Bataan*.

**December 9**: 20th Century-Fox announces that Jennifer Jones, an unknown actress under contract to Selznick, has been signed to portray Saint Bernadette.

1943 **March 9**: Filming on *Song of Bernadette* begins.

**July 25**: Principal photography on *Bernadette* completed.

**September 8**: Filming begins on *Since You Went Away*.

**October**:  Jennifer Jones and Robert Walker separate.

**December 27**: *Song of Bernadette* premiers.

1944   **February 9**:  Filming on *Since You Went Away* completed.

**February 25**:  Makes personal appearance in Tulsa for nationwide premier of *Song of Bernadette*.

**March 2**:  Awarded Oscar as Best Actress of 1943.

**March 3**:  Files for divorce from actor Robert Walker.

**June**:  *Since You Went Away* premiers.

1945   **February 28**:  Filming begins on *Duel in the Sun*.

**March 15**:  Loses best supporting actress Oscar to Ethel Barrymore.

**June 20**:  Is granted divorce from Robert Walker.

**August 24**:  David O. Selznick and his wife, Irene Mayer, separate.

**November**:  Filming on *Duel in the Sun* completed.

**December 3**:  Filming begins on *Cluny Brown*, directed by Ernst Lubitsch.

1946   **March 7**:  Loses best actress Oscar to Joan Crawford.

**December 30:**  *Duel in the Sun* premiers in Los Angeles.

1947   **March 13**:  Loses best actress Oscar to Olivia de Havilland.

**May**:  *Duel in the Sun* opens nationwide.

**February**:  Location filming begins in New York City on *Portrait of Jennie*, then shuts down.

**April**:  Location filming resumes.

**November**:  New York filming completed; Irene Mayer Selznick files for divorce.

1948   **January**:  The David Selznick/Irene Mayer Selznick divorce finalized.

**November**:  Robert Walker committed to sanitarium in Topeka,

Kansas.

1949 **March 29**: *Portrait of Jennie* premiers in New York.

**July 13**: Marries David O. Selznick off the coast of Italy.

**August**: Begins filming *Gone to Earth* in England with Michael Powell directing.

1950 **July**: Begins filming *Carrie* for director William Wyler.

**August**: Louella O. Parsons hints in gossip column that Jennifer is pregnant; she denies the rumor.

**November**: Filming on *Carrie* completed.

**December 16**: Suffers miscarriage.

1951 **May**: Travels to Japan and Korea to visit wounded American soldiers.

**August 28**: Robert Walker dies.

1952 **March**: Begins filming *Ruby Gentry*.

**May**: *Gone to Earth* is released in America under the title *The Wild Heart*.

**June**: *Carrie* opens.

**December**: Begins filming *Indiscretion of an American Wife* in Italy; *Ruby Gentry* opens.

1953 Films *Beat the Devil* in Italy under direction of John Huston.

1954 **February**: Accepts offer to star in Paramount's *The Country Girl*, but is forced to withdraw due to pregnancy.

**June**: *Indiscretion of an American Wife* opens to poor reviews.

**August 12**: Mary Jennifer Selznick born.

**December 21**: Makes Broadway debut in *Portrait of a Lady*; reviews poor; play closes after seven performances.

1955 Films *Love is Many-Splendored Thing*, *Good Morning, Miss Dove* and *The Man in the Gray Flannel Suit*.

1956  **March 21**: Loses best actress Oscar to Anna Magnani.

June:  Begins filming *The Barretts of Wimpole Street* in London.

1957  **February**: *The Barretts of Wimpole Street* opens;  filming begins in Italy on *A Farewell to Arms*.

September: Filming completed.

**December 19**:  *Farewell* premiers in Los Angeles; reviews not good.

1961  **May**: Filming begins in Europe on *Tender is the Night*.

1962  **February 1**: *Tender is the Night* released; reviews mixed.

1964  **April**: Selznick suffers first of a series of heart attacks.

1965  **March:** Appears on stage in Palm Beach and Miami, Florida, in *The Man With the Perfect Wife*.

**June 23**: David O. Selznick dies at age 63.

November: Takes over for an ill Kim Stanley in film *The Idol*.

1966  **August 1**: *The Idol* released; reviews poor.

**September 29**:  Opens in *The Country Girl* at New York's City Center for limited engagement.

1967  **November 9**:  Found in surf at Malibu, still alive after suicide attempt.

1969  **February 17**:  Begins filming *Angel, Angel Down We Go*.

**May 29**:  Flora Mae Isley dies in Dallas.

**July**:  Filming completed.

**August**:  Film released and mercilessly panned.

1971  **May 5**:  Meets millionaire Norton Simon at Annenberg party.

**May 30**:  Married Norton Simon aboard yacht in English Channel.

1974  **Spring**:  Begins filming character part in *The Towering Inferno*.

**December 10**:  Film premiers.

1976 **May 11**: Mary Jennifer Selznick jumps to her death from the roof of a Los Angeles hotel, age 21.

**May 27**: Phil Isley dies in Dallas.

1977 **September**: Named chairman of the directors of the Norton Simon Museum.

1980 **April 15**: Bids the then-record sum of 3.74 million dollars for Dutch painting of the Resurrection of Christ.

1984 **March**: Appears on the televised AFI tribute to Lillian Gish.

**May**: Norton Simon striken with Guillian-Barre Syndrome, a debilitating muscle disorder.

1987 **March 30**: Presents Oscar for Best Cinematography but appears nervous and ill at ease.

1989 **March 10:** Simon relinquishes control of his museum to his wife.

**March 19**: Appears on the televised AFI tribute to Gregory Peck.

# 3
# *Filmography*

## F1  NEW FRONTIER (A Republic Production)

Released: Aug. 10, 1939                           Running Time: 56 minutes

**Cast:**
John Wayne, Ray Corrigan, Raymond Hatton (The Three Mesquiteers);
Phylis Isley (Celia Braddock); Eddy Waller (Major Steven Braddock);
Sammy McKim (Stevie Braddock); LeRoy Mason (Gilbert); Harrison
Greene (Assemblyman William Potter); Reginald Barlow (Judge Bill
Lawson); Burr Caruth (Doc William Hall); Dave O'Brien (Jason Braddock);
Hal Price (Sheriff).

**Credits:**
Director (George Sherman); Associate Producer (William Berke); Editor
(Tony Martinelli); Cinematographer (Reggie Lanning); Screenplay (Betty
Burbridge, Luci Ward).

**Synoposis:**
When the Civil War ends, pioneers head west to settle new lands.  Major
Braddock settles in a valley which he names New Hope.  Fifty years later,
having out lived most of his fellow settlers, he is on hand for the town's half-
century celebration and brings his granddaughter, Celia, to the dance where
she meets Stony, leader of the Three Mesquiteers.  The feeling of hope and
prosperity which the little valley has known for fifty years is suddenly
destroyed when the state legislature announces that the valley will become a
resevoir.  The residents of the valley, led by Major Braddock and his son,
Jason, vow to delay construction of the dam and to fight for their valley. The
Three Mesquiteers join the fight, as do Celia and her small brother, Stevie.  A
violent fight ensues between the ranchers and the dishonest men behind the
construction company, and the Three Mesquiteers are arrested.  It appears
that the government has won and the ranchers begin their trek to new land
where they will be re-located, but that land is dry and arid. The Three

Mesquiteers break out of their cell, and another fight erupts at the dam site. The flood gate is accidently opened and Celia runs to avoid being swept away by the rising water. Gilbert, one of the evil owners of the construction company, is drowned before Stony can close the flood gate. The others involved in the scheme are tried on land fraud charges and sentenced to ten years. A feeling of hope and prosperity returns to the valley.

**Review Summary:**
*Variety* (August 16, 1939) noted the debut of Phylis Isley, but thought the role didn't "give her a good chance."

The *New York Daily News* (September 10, 1939) termed Phylis Isley a "cute new girl."

**Additional Sources:**
Reviews: *New York Journal American*, September 10, 1939; *Film Daily*, September 7, 1939.


F2    **DICK TRACY'S G MEN** (A Republic Production)

15-chapter serial.                     First chapter released Sept. 2, 1939

**Cast:**
Ralph Byrd (Dick Tracy); Irving Pichel (Nicholas Zarnoff); Ted Pearson (Steve Lockwood); Phylis Isley (Gwen Andrews); Walter Miller (Robal); George Douglas (Sandoval); Kenneth Harlan (Clive Anderson); Robert Carson (Scott); Julian Madison (Foster); Ted Mapes (Ted Murchison); William Stahl (Bruce); Robert Wayne (Wilbur); Joe McGuinn (Tom); Ken Terrell (Ed Hardy); Sammy McKim (Sammy Williams).

**Credits:**
Directors (William Witney, John English); Associate Producer (Robert Beche); Screenplay (Barry Shipman, Franklyn Adreon, Rex Taylor, Ronald Davidson, Sol Shor); Editor (William Nobles); Musical Score (William Lava).

**Synopsis:**
Dick Tracy and Steve, his assistant, battle the evil criminal Zarnoff, who attempts to blow up the Great Industrial Canal, murder President Huenemo Mendoza, steal $2,500,000 in gold bullion and smuggle stolen documents across the border. Tracy keeps track of Zarnoff's movements by having messages relayed from the FBI office by his secretary, Gwen Andrews. The evil Zarnoff, in an attempt to steal military plans for an aerial torpedo, is finally felled not by Tracy, but by drinking arsenic-laced water from a desert watering hole.

**Review Summary:**
No reviews were published in the usual sources.

## F3   THE SONG OF BERNADETTE   (A 20th Century-Fox Production)

Released: December 27, 1943                    Running Time: 157 minutes

**Cast:**
Jennifer Jones (Bernadette Soubirous); Charles Bickford (Dean Peyramale); William Eythe (Antoine Nicolau); Vincent Price (Prosecutor Dutour); Lee J. Cobb (Dr. Dozous); Gladys Cooper (Sister Marie Theresa Vauzous); Anne Revere (Louise Soubirous); Roman Bohnen (Francois Soubirous); Mary Anderson (Jeanne Abadie); Aubrey Mather (Mayor Lacade); Charles Dingle (Commissioner Jacomet); Edith Barrett (Croisine Bouhouhorts); Sig Ruman (Louis Bouriette); Ermadean Walters (Marie Soubirous); Patricia Morison (Empress Eugenie); Jerome Cowan (Emperor Napoleon); Marcel Dalio (Policeman Callet); Blanche Yurka (Aunt Bernarde Casteret); Pedro de Cordoba (Dr. Le Crampe); Moroni Olson (Chaplain); Nana Bryant (Convent Mother Superior); Linda Darnell ("The Lady").

**Credits:**
Director (Henry King); Producer (William Perlberg); Music (Alfred Newman); Screenplay (George Seaton, from novel by Franz Werfel); Photography (Arthur Miller, ASC); Art Direction (James Basevi, William Darling); Set Decorations (Thomas Little); Editor (Barbara McLean); Costumes (Rene Hubert); Special Effects (Fred Sersen).

**Synopsis:**
On a cold winter day, Bernadette Soubirous, a 14-year-old asthmatic, accompanies her sister and a friend on a wood-gathering expedition. She lingers behind the others, and in a grotto, near the village, she is started by a light coming from a niche in the rocks behind her. Then before her appears a vision of "The Lady" dressed in all white, who instructs Bernadette to return to the grotto every day for fifteen days. The town learns of Bernadette's strange vision and the mayor is concerned that it will prevent the railroad from coming through Lourdes. She is pressured to admit that she had made up the story, but she remains streadfast. To prove the validity of Berna-dette's story, the local dean asks her to have "The Lady" make the rose bush in the grotto bloom. A large crowd follows her to watch, and although the rose does not bloom,"The Lady" instructs Bernadette to eat the leaves of plants nearby and wash herself there. She doesn't find water, but scrubs her body with dirt. The townspeople think she is derranged and lead her away, but after she has gone, water springs from the spot where she had dug, and when a blind man washes his face, he can suddenly see. A miracle is

proclaimed and crowds come to the "healing pool." The church continues to doubt Bernadette's story they conduct examinations that drag on for five years, after which she becomes a nun, still telling the same simple story. She eventually contracts tuberculosis of the bone, but refuses to visit the healing pool before her death.

**Review Summary:**
*The Hollywood Reporter* (December 22, 1943) found Jennifer Jones's performance moving and sincere, capturing the "essential spirit of Bernadette Soubirous" with never a false note. Her interpretation was described as often transcending acting, reflecting an internal beauty and serenity.

*The New Yorker* (January 29, 1944), thought that Jennifer Jones was not the "find of the decade," but admitted to not finding any "noticeable mistakes" in her performance.

**Additional Sources:**
Reviews: *Commonweal*, February 11, 1944; *Film Daily*, December 27, 1943; *Motion Picture Herald Product Digest*, December 25, 1943; *The Nation*, January 29, 1944; *The New Republic*, March 6, 1944; *The New York Times*, January 27, 1944; *Newsweek*, February 7, 1944; *Saturday Review*, February 19, 1944; *Time*, February 7, 1944; *Variety*, December 22, 1943.
See Also: *Agee on Film*, Volume 1; *Around Cinemas*; *Magills Survey of Cinema*, Series 1; *Vincent Price Unmasked*.

**Notes:**
*The Song of Bernadette* was nominated for twelve Academy Awards: Best Picture; Best Actress (Jones); Best Supporting Actor (Bickford); Best Supporting Actress (Cooper and Revere); Best Director; Best Screenplay; Black and White Cinematography; Black and White Interior Decoration; Sound Recording; Best Scoring; and Best Film Editing. The film was awarded four of those Oscars: Best Actress, Cinematography, Interior Decoration and Score.

F4   **SINCE YOU WENT AWAY** (A United Artists Production)

Released: July 20, 1944                              Running Time: 172 minutes

**Cast:**
Claudette Colbert (Anne Hilton); Jennifer Jones (Jane Hilton); Joseph Cotten (Lieut. Tony Willett); Shirley Temple (Bridget Hilton); Monty Woolley (Colonel Smollett); Lionel Barrymore (Clergyman); Robert Walker (Corp. Bill Smollett); Hattie McDaniel (Fidelia); Agnes Moorehead (Emily Hawkins); Nazimova (Mrs. Koslowska, welder); Albert Basserman (Dr.

Sigmund Golden); Gordon Oliver (Marine Officer); Keenan Wynn (Lieut. Solomon); Guy Madison (Harold Smith); Craig Stevens (Danny Williams); Lloyd Corrigan (Mr. Mahoney); Jackie Moran (Johnny Mahoney); Jane Devlin (Gladys Brown); George Chandler (Taxi Driver); Florence Bates (Hungry Woman, on train); Irving Bacon (Bartender); Addison Richards (Maj. Sam Atkins); Barbara Pepper (Pin Girl); Adeline de Walt Reynolds (Elderly Woman, on train); Ann Gillis (Becky Anderson); Dorothy Garner (Sugar); Andrew McLaglen (Former Plowboy); Jill Warren (Waitress); Terry Moore (Refugee Child); Robert Johnson (Negro Officer); Dorothy Dandridge (Negro Officer's Wife); Jonathan Hale (Conductor); Ruth Roman (An Envious Girl); Grady Sutton (Corporal, at dance); Rhonda Fleming (Girl, at dance).

**Credits:**
Director (John Cromwell); Producer, Screenplay (David O. Selznick); Photography (Lee Garmes, ASC, Stanley Cortez, ASC); Music (Max Steiner); Interior Decoration (Victor A. Gangelin); Supervising Film Editor (Hal C. Kern); Associate Film Editor (James E. Newcom); Special Effects (Jack Cosgrove).

**Synopsis:**
Returning home after seeing her captain husband off on active duty, Anne Hilton realizes that economy measures must be taken if the family is to live within the wartime restrictions. Bridget suggests they take in a roomer, and so old, crochety Colonel Smollett moves into the guest bedroom. Tony Willett, a friend of the family, also moves in for a while and Jane develops a crush for him. Tony eventually departs for active duty and Jane is drawn more and more to the shy and somewhat withdrawn Bill Smollett, the grandson of their border, who was discharged from Westpoint, but who has become a corporal in the army. After graduation from high school, Jane becomes a nurse's aid in a rehabilitation ward aiding amputees and wounded veterans. She has grown still closer to the shy Bill Smollett, and before his midnight train which will take him into active duty, they spend the afternoon in the country where, during a rainstorm, they reveal their feelings for one another and make plans to be married. They write often and make plans for the future, but word comes that he has been killed in Salerno. Anne begins to feel that she should have a hand in the war effort, so she trains as a lady welder. On Christmas Eve, with the house full of family and friends, Anne receives a call telling her that her husband is not only alive (he had been reported missing in action) but that he is coming home on furlough.

**Review Summary:**
*Time* (July 17, 1944) praised Selznick for bringing Jones "out of the cloister" and making her an All-American girl. Her performance was termed "nervous, carefully studied and overly intense."

Bosley Crowther, writing for *The New York Times* (July 21, 1944) found

Jennifer "surpassingly sweet" as the typical American daughter on the threshold of womanhood, enjoying her first love.

**Additional Sources:**
Reviews: *Commonweal*, August 4, 1944; *Film Daily*, July 19, 1944; *Hollywood Reporter*, July 19, 1944; *Life*, July 24, 1944; *The London Times*, January 11, 1945; *Motion Picture Exhibitor*, July 26, 1944; *Motion Pictrure Herald Product Digest*, July 22, 1944; *The Nation*, July 29, 1944; *The New Republic*, July 17, 1944; *New Yorker*, July 29, 1944; *Newsweek*, July 10, 1944; *Saturday Review*, July 29, 1944; *Scholastic*, September 11, 1944; *Theatre Arts*, September, 1944; *Variety*, July 19, 1944.
See Also: *Agee on Film*, Volume 1; *Films and Filming*, October, 1981; *The Films of the Second World War*; *The Films of Shirley Temple*; *The Films of World War II*; *Magic Moments of the Movies*; *Magills Survey of Cinema*, Series II; *Selected Film Criticism 1941-1950*; *Women's Film and the Female Experience*.

**Notes:**
*Since You Went Away* was nominated for nine Academy Awards: Best Film; Best Actress (Colbert); Best Supporting Actor (Woolley); Best Supporting Actress (Jones); Cinematography; Special Effects; Interior Decoration; Best Score; and Film Editing. The film won only one Oscar, for Max Steiner's musical score.

## F5   LOVE LETTERS (A Paramount Production)

Released: October 26, 1945                    Running Time: 101 minutes

**Cast:**
Jennifer Jones (Singleton); Joseph Cotten (Alan Quinton); Ann Richards (Dilly Carson); Cecil Kellaway (Mack); Gladys Cooper (Beatrice Remington); Anita Louise (Helen Wentworth); Robert Sully (Roger Morland); Reginald Denny (Defense Attorney); Ernest Cossart (Bishop); Byron Barr (Derek Quinton); James Millican (Jim Connings); Lumsden Hare (Mr. Quinton); Winifred Harris (Mrs. Quinton); Ethel May Halls (Bishop's Wife); Matthew Boulton (Judge); David Clyde (Postman); Ian Wolfe (Vicar); Alec Craig (Dodd); Arthur Hohl (Jupp); Conrad Binyon (Boy in Library); Nina Borget (Barmaid in Italian Inn); Mary Field (Nurse); Constance Purdy (Old Hag).

**Credits:**
Director (William Dieterle); Producer (Hal Wallis); Screenplay (Ayn Rand); Photography (Lee Garmes, ASC); Art Direction (Hans Dreier, Roland Anderson); Music Score (Victor Young); Set Decoration (Ray Moyer);

Costumes (Edith Head); Editor (Anne Bauchens); Special Effects (Gordon Jennings, ASC).

**Synopsis:**
In Italy, Alan writes letters to Victoria for Roger, a friend who feels that he is unable to put his thoughts onto paper. Victoria falls in love with Roger because of the letters and marries him. A few years later Alan later learns that Roger is dead, and he meets a strange young woman named Singleton who tells him she has no past and no other name. He realizes that he is love with Victoria, to whom he wrote the bogus letters, and tries to track her down; he learns that her husband, Roger, was murdered and that she had been accused of the crime and had been sentenced to a year in prison. He also learns through a friend that Victoria and Singleton are the same person, and that since the murder, she has had no memory other than her childhood and the present. It seems that when Roger was discovered murdered, she was found with the knife in her hand and blood on her dress. Her elderly aunt, who had suffered a stroke, could only mutter "He struck her." Alan's love for Victoria has not dimished, and they marry and live a happy life in the country. One day, while on a drive, they happen upon the desolate farm where the murder had occurred. She begins to remember the details, and her aunt, who has recovered from the stroke, is finally able to tell what happened. Roger had attacked Victoria and it was the aunt who killed him, to protect her niece, but was felled by a stroke and couldn't defend the helpless girl against the charges of murder. Alan admits that it was he who wrote the letters, and happiness returns to their lives.

**Review Summary:**
According to *Variety* (August 22, 1945), Jennifer Jones "gathers new kudos" for her performance as Singleton.

*The New York Times* (August 27, 1945) was not enthusiastic, predicting that Jennifer's reputation as a fine actress would "suffer a terrible dent" due to her "fatuous" performance in the film, but did admit that a bad script and poor direction might be to blame.

**Additional Sources:**
Reviews: *Commonweal*, August 24, 1945; *Film Daily,* August 20, 1945; *Hollywood Reporter*, August 20, 1945; *Life*, September 24, 1945; *The Nation*, September 29, 1945; *The New Republic*, October 8, 1945; *The New Yorker*, September 8, 1945; *Newsweek*, September 3, 1945; *Time*, September 10, 1945.

**Notes:**
Despite mixed reviews, Jennifer Jones was nominated for her third consecutive Academy Award. She lost the Best Actress Oscar to Joan Crawford.

## F6    CLUNY BROWN (A 20th Century-Fox Production)

Released: June 1946                    Running Time: 100 Minutes

**Cast:**
Charles Boyer (Adam Belinski); Jennifer Jones (Cluny Brown); Peter Lawford (Andrew Carmel); Helen Walker (Betty Cream); Reginald Gardiner (Hilary Ames); Sir C. Aubrey Smith (Col. Duff Graham); Richard Haydn (Wilson); Margaret Bannerman (Lady Alice Carmel); Sara Allgood (Mrs. Maile); Ernest Cossart (Syrette); Florence Bates (Dowager); Una O'Connor (Mrs. Wilşon); Queenie Leonard (Weller); Billy Bevan (Uncle Arn); Michael Dyne (John Frewen); Christopher Severn (Master Snaffle); Rex Evans (Guest Piano Player); Harold DeBecker (Mr. Snaffle); Jean Prescott (Mrs. Snaffle); Ottola Nesmith (Mrs. Tupham); Al Winters (Rollins); Charles Coleman (Constable Birkins); Billy Gray (Boy in Shop).

**Credits:**
Director, Producer (Ernst Lubitsch); Screenplay (Samuel Hoffenstein, Elizabeth Reinhardt, based on the novel by Margery Sharp); Photography (Joseph LaShelle, ASC); Art Direction (Lyle Wheeler, Russell Spencer); Music (Cyril Mockridge); Film Editor (Dorothy Spencer); Special Effects (Fred Sersen).

**Synopsis:**
With a stopped-up sink and guests expected for cocktails, Hilary Ames puts in a call to Arn Brown, a plumber who is willing to work on Sundays. In the meantime, Adam Belinski arrives and is mistaken for the plumber, but finally Cluny arrives, explaining that she had taken the call for her uncle, and proceeds to unstop the drain. Later, when she is sent to the Carmel Manor as a maid, she is at first mistaken for a debutante. Her identity is eventually found out and she begins work as the new maid. Adam Belinski arrives as a guest, he and Cluny recognize each other, and become friendly. Belinski is obviously taken with Cluny, but she becomes engaged to prissy Mr. Wilson, the village chemist. Plans for their marriage fail when, at Mrs. Wilson's birthday party, the drain stops up and Cluny, ever the plumber's niece, promptly unstops it, to the stern disapproval of the Wilsons. Cluny, upset and bewildered, takes to her bed, and although Belinski tries to see her, he is not allowed into her room. He has a present delivered to her, which touches her and she races after him to the train station where he is about to leave on a trip. She joins him on the train, and throws her maid's cap and uniform out the window.

**Review Summary:**
*The Hollywood Reporter* (May 1, 1946) thought Jennifer Jones "magnificent" in her first comedy role. Her talent was termed "electric" and her acting "superb."

*Variety* (May 1, 1946) praised Jennifer's interpretation of Cluny, making her a "delightful character who will immediately catch on with the audience."

**Additional Sources:**
Reviews: *Commonweal*, June 14, 1946; *Film Daily*, May 1, 1946; *Life*, May 27, 1946; *Motion Picture Herald Product Digest*, April 27, 1946; *The Nation*, June 8, 1946; *The New Republic*, July 29, 1946; *The New York Times*, June 3, 1946; *The New Yorker*, June 15, 1946; *Newsweek*, May 6, 1946; *Sight and Sound*, August, 1946; *Theatre Arts*, June, 1946; *Time*, May 20, 1946.
See Also: *Agee on Film*, Volume 1; *The Cinema of Ernst Lubitsch*; *Ernst Lubitsch's American Comedy*; *Magills Survey of Cinema*, Series II.

**Notes:**
*Cluny Brown* was the last completed motion picture of Ernst Lubitsch, who died the following year in the middle of filming *The Lady in Ermine* with Betty Grable.

F7   **DUEL IN THE SUN**   (A Selznick Production)

Released: December 31, 1946                   Running Time: 138 minutes

**Cast:**
Jennifer Jones (Pearl Chavez); Joseph Cotten (Jesse McCanless); Gregory Peck (Lewt McCanless); Lionel Barrymore (Senator McCanless); Lillian Gish (Laura Belle McCanless); Walter Huston (Jubal Crabbe); Charles Bickford (Sam Pierce); Herbert Marshall (Scott Chavez); Harry Carey (Lem Smoot); Joan Tetzel (Helen Langford); Tilly Losch (Mrs. Chavez); Butterfly McQueen (Vashti); Scott McKay (Sid); Otto Kruger (Mr. Langford); Sidney Blackmer (The Lover); Charles Dingle (Sheriff Thompson); Dan White (Ed); Steve Dunhill (Jake); Frank Cordell (Ken); Francis McDonald, Victor Kilian (Gamblers); Griff Barnett (Jailer); Lane Chandler (Capt. U.S. Cavalry); Kermit Maynard (Barfly, Presidio Bar); Bert Roach (An Eater).

**Credits:**
Director (King Vidor); Screenplay (David O. Selznick, from the novel by Niven Busch); Photography (Lee Garmes, Hal Rosson, Ray Rennahan, ASC); Music (Dimitri Tiomkin); Art Direction (James Basevi); Interior Decoration (Emile Kuri); Color Director (Natalie Kalmus); Sound Director (James G. Stewart);  Special Effects (Clarence Slifer, Jack Cosgrove).

**Synopsis:**
Scott Chavez, an aristocratic Southern gentleman, shocked by the wanton actions of his Indian wife, kills her and her lover, but before being hanged for the crime, arranges for his daughter, Pearl, to be taken in by his cousin's

family, headed by Senator McCanless. She arrives at the McCanless ranch, Spanish Bit, and immediately sparks a flame of lust in Lewt, one of two McCanless brothers. She at first tries to resist him, but soon gives in to his animal magnetism. The other brother, Jesse, takes the side of the railroad company who wants to lay tracks across part of the McCanless ranch, and the Senator tells him to leave, but before he does, he, too, confesses to Pearl that he loves her. Lewt and Pearl then become lovers and everyone assumes they will be married, but Lewt admits to his father that he is merely toying with Pearl. She realizes Lewt's affection isn't true, and agrees to marry Sam Pierce, but Lewt shoots him down. Instead of turning him over to the authorities, the Senator gives Lewt money and tells him to hide in Mexico. Laura Belle becomes ill and dies, and Jesse, returning to see his mother, invites Pearl to come live with him and the woman he is about to marry. Lewt hears of this, confronts his brother and shoots him. Pearl nurses Jesse until Helen comes to take over, then she asks one of Lewt's friends where he is hiding. She rides out in search of Squaw's Head Rock, and when Lewt shows himself, Pearl takes aim and fires. Lewt returns fire, hitting his lover, and the two crawl toward each other and die in a bloody embrace.

**Review Summary:**
*The New York Times* (May 8, 1947) thought that, at times, she accurately portrayed the "pathos of loneliness and heartbreak" that Pearl Chavez felt, but thought her performance on the whole as a passion-run child of nature was in the "loosest theatrical style."

*Look* (June 10, 1947) didn't particularly like the film, but thought Jennifer Jones gave "arresting vigor to the sordid romance."

**Additional Sources:**
Reviews: *Commonweal*, May 23, 1947; *Film Daily*, December 31, 1946; *Hollywood Reporter*, December 31, 1946; *Life*, October, 1947; *Motion Picture Herald Product Digest*, January 11, 1947; *The New Republic*, May 19, 1947; *Newsweek*, March 3, 1947; *Theatre Arts*, June, 1947; *Time*, January 27, 1947, March 17, 1947; *Variety*, January 1, 1947.
See Also: *The Filming of the West*; *The Films of Gregory Peck*; *King Vidor on Filmmaking*; *Magills Survey of Cinema*, Series II; *The Making of the Great Westerns*; *Selected Film Criticism 1941-50*; *A Tree is a Tree*.

**Notes:**
A $2 million dollar promotional campaign for this massive film included dropping 5,000 parachutes at the Kentucky Derby and beach stickers which spelled out the film's title on sunburned skin.

F8   **PORTRAIT OF JENNIE** (A Selznick Production)

Released: April 21, 1949                    Running Time: 86 minutes

**Cast:**
Jennifer Jones (Jennie Appleton); Joseph Cotten (Eben Adams); Ethel
Barrymore (Miss Spinney); Cecil Kellaway (Mr. Matthews); Lillian Gish
(Sister Mary of Mercy); David Wayne (Gus O'Toole); Albert Sharp (Mr.
Moore); Henry Hull (Eke); Florence Bates (Mrs. Jekes); Maude Simmons
(Clara Morgan); Felix Bressart (The Doorman); Clem Bevans (Captain
Caleb Cobb); Esther Somers (Mrs. Bunce); John Farrell (Policeman); Robert
Dudley (Mariner); Anne Francis (Girl in Museum).

**Credits:**
Director (William Dieterle); Producer (David O. Selznick); Screenplay
(Paul Osborn, Perter Berneis, from the novel by Robert Nathan); Associate
Producer (David Hempstead); Music (Dimitri Tiomkin, based upon themes
of Claude Debussy); Photography (Joseph August, ASC); Costumes
(Lucinda Ballard); Special Effects (Clarence Slifer).

**Synopsis:**
During the cold, grim winter of 1934, Eben Adams, a down-on-his-luck
artist, finally manages to sell a painting to crusty old Miss Spinney, owner of
an art gallery, and on his way home, cutting through Central Park, he meets
Jennie, a strange little girl who tells him her parents are high-wire
performers at Hammerstein's Victoria, although Adams knows that
Hammerstein's was torn down years before. Before disappearing into the
night, the little girl asks the artist to wait for her until she grows up. He
sketches the little girl and sells it to Miss Spinney for $25. A week or so later,
he meets Jennie again in the park, but she has grown taller, older. She says
three years have gone by, and that she is hurrying to grow up. They make a
date to meet, and when Jennie doesn't show up, he begins tracing the girl's
history. From people who worked at Hammerstein's, he learns that the
Appleton's were indeed high-wire performers, but were killed in a fall many
years before. No one knew what had happened to their pretty daughter,
Jennie. He sees a picture of Jennie Appleton and recognizes the girl from the
park. He sees her again in the park and finds her crying over her parent's
death, but he consoles her and although she tells him she will be attending a
convent, makes him promise to wait for her. Weeks pass and he doesn't see
her, so he begins to capture her spiritual quality on canvas. He finds that he is
slowly falling in love with the mysterious girl. One day he finds her in his
apartment, and the next day he meets her at the convent where they watch
girls taking the veil. He sees her again, soon after, and she tells him that she
has graduated but will be going away to Cape Cod for the summer. Adams
visits the convent where Sister Mary of Mercy tells him that Jennie died years
ago in a New England hurricane. On the anniversary of Jennie's death, he
goes out to the Lands End lighthouse at Cape Cod, where Jennie had loved to
sail, and is caught there in a fierce storm. Over the noise of the wind and
waves, he hears Jennie calling to him. They embrace and Adams tries to get

her to the light house, but she tells him it is useless, that she must die, but that they will never be separated. A huge wave snatches her from his arms and she is gone. But though he has lost Jennie, he gains fame for his "Portrait of Jennie" which hangs in a New York art museum.

**Review Summary:**
*The Hollywood Reporter* (December 24, 1948) thought Jennifer Jones gave a "sensitive, appealing performance" but added that the film never really comes to life.

*Variety* (December 29, 1948) said that Jennifer's talents were "showcased inspiringly" as the ethereal Jennie.

**Additional Sources:**
Reviews: *Colliers*, February 5, 1949; *Commonweal*, April 1, 1949; *Film Daily*, December 30, 1948; *Motion Picture Herald Product Digest*, January 1, 1949; *The New York Times*, March 30, 1949; *The New Yorker*, April 29, 1949; *Newsweek*, April 4, 1949; *Time*, April 4, 1949.
See Also: *Magills Survey of Cinema*, Series I.

**Notes:**
*Portrait of Jennie* was a failure in its day, the first for Jennifer Jones, but in the four decades since its release, it has found its place in the hearts of dedicated filmgoers, and is often listed among the favorites of noted film historians. Clarence Slifer's special effects won an Oscar.

## F9    WE WERE STRANGERS (A Columbia Pictures Production)

Released: April 22, 1949                          Running Time: 106 minutes

**Cast:**
Jennifer Jones (China Valdez); John Garfield (Tony Fenner); Pedro Armendariz (Armando Ariete); Gilbert Roland (Guillermo); Ramon Novarro (Chief); Wally Cassell (Miguel); David Bond (Ramon); Jose Perez (Toto); Morris Ankrum (Mr. Seymore, Bank Manager); Tito Renaldo (Manolo); Paul Monte (Roberto); Leonard Strong (Bombmaker); Robert Tafur (Rubio); Alexander McSweyn, Alfonso Pedroza (Sanitation Men); Ted Hecht (Enrico); Santiago Martinez (Waiter); Joel Rene (Student); Argentina Brunetti (Mama); Robert Malcolm (Priest); Roberta Haynes (Lolita); Lelia Goldoni (Consuelo); Paul Marion (Truck Driver); Mimi Aguglia (Mama); Felipe Turich (Spy); John Huston (Bank Teller).
**Credits:**
Director (John Huston); Producer (S.P. Eagle); Associate Producer (Jules Buck); Screenplay (Peter Viertel, John Huston); Photography (Russell Metty, ASC); Art Director (Cary Odell); Film Editor (Al Clark); Set Decoration

(Louis Diage); Costumes (Jean Louis); Musical Score (George Antheil); Musical Director (M.W. Stoloff).

**Synopsis:**
The Cuban Senate in 1933 passes a law prohibiting public gatherings of more than four persons, and a resistance movement springs up in opposition. Manolo, one of a group of young people who speak out against the government, is gunned down by Ariete, head of the secret police, as his sister, China, watches. Spurred by this inhuman act, she joins the movement against the government and meets Tony Fenner, a Cuban American working for the resistance. He tells China of his plan to rid Cuba of the evil Presidente and his government followers, and she agrees to help him dig a tunnel from her house to the tomb of an important government official. They will assassinate the official, and at his funeral, explode a bomb that will kill the other government officials who are attending. As their project gets underway, the realize they are falling in love, and one night, with Tony listening in the tunnel below, Ariete pays China a visit and tries to force himself on her. He fires a gun, but the noise only alerts his bodyguard who takes him away. The assassination is carried out successfully and everything is set for the explosion at the funeral, but the family of the dead man decide to take his body elsewhere for burial, and through China's attempt to cash a check for Tony at the bank where she works, Ariete learns of their anti-government activities. He traps them in China's house, firing at them. Tony is hit and dies in China's arms, but at the moment of his death, bells begin ringing, annoucing the uprising of the population. Ariete is killed and the Presidente is forced to flee for his life. Tony did not live to see the victory, but China knows that his sacrifice was not in vain.

**Review Summary:**
*The New York Times* (April 24, 1949) thought much was lacking in the performance of Jennifer Jones. According to the reviewer, she achieved neither "understanding nor passion" in her interpretation.

*Variety* (April 27, 1949) commented on Jennifer's lack of elaborate costuming and make-up, her "neat Cuban accent," and found her performance "excellent" and "effective."

**Other Sources:**
Reviews: *Commonweal*, May 6, 1949; *Cue*, April 30, 1949; *Film Daily*, April 21, 1949; *Film Bulletin*, June 6, 1949; *Hollywood Reporter*, April 22, 1949; *Motion Picture Herald Product Digest*, April 30, 1949; *The New Republic*, May 5, 1949; *The New York Herald Tribune*, April 28, 1949; *The New York Journal of Commerce*, April 29, 1949; *The New Yorker*, May 7, 1949; *Newsweek*, May 9, 1949; *Rotarian*, October, 1949; *Sequence*, August, 1949; *Sunday Mirror Magazine*, April 3, 1949; *Theatre Arts*, May, 1949; *Time*, May 2, 1949.
See Also: *The Films of John Garfield*; *The Films of John Huston*.

## F10   **MADAME BOVARY** (A Metro-Goldwyn-Mayer Picture)

Released: August 27, 1949                              Running Time: 106 minutes

**Cast:**
Jennifer Jones (Emma Bovary); Van Heflin (Charles Bovary); Louis Jourdan (Rodolphe Boulanger); James Mason (Gustave Flaubert); Christopher Kent (Leon Dupuis); Gene Lockhart (J. Homais); Frank Allenby (Lhereux); Gladys Cooper (Mme. Dupuis); John Abbott (Mayor Tuvache); Henry Morgan (Hyppolite); George Zucco (Dobocage); Ellen Corby (Felicite); Eduard Franz (Roualt); Henri Letondal (Guillaumin); Esther Somers (Mme. Lefrancois); Frederic Tozere (Pinard); Paul Cavanagh (Marquis D'Andervilliers); Larry Simms (Justin); Edith Evanson (Mother Superior).

**Credits:**
Director (Vincente Minelli); Producer (Pandro S. Berman); Screenplay (Robert Ardrey, from the novel by Gustave Flaubert); Photography (Robert Planck, ASC); Music (Miklos Rozsa); Art Director (Cedric Gibbons, Jack Martin Smith); Film Editor (Ferris Webster); Special Effects (Warren Newcombe).

**Synopsis:**
Gustave Flaubert, on trial for writing an immoral novel, defends Emma Bovary, and begins her story on a stormy night when Dr. Bovary is summoned to the Roualt farm to set the owner's broken leg.  In due time, the doctor proposes to Roualt's daughter, Emma, and, longing to leave the farm, she accepts.  They settle in Yonville where Emma entertains rather poorly and over-extends her husband's credit.  She wishes for a son, but gives birth to a daughter.  Bored with her life in Yonville, she is particularly attracted to handsome Rodolphe Boulanger whom she meets at an elegant ball.  She returns to her dreary life and has an affair with Leon, a draper, but he is called away to Paris, and she begins having an affair with Rodolphe, whom she meets again by chance. She is soon hopelessly in love and begs Rodolphe to take her away from Yonville, but on the night she plans to run away with him, he sends her a note telling her he has decided to go to Italy alone.  The desparately unhappy Emma tries to throw herself out of a second story window, but Charles saves her in time.  She loses interest in life, but happens to meet her old lover, Leon, at an opera and is delighted when he confesses his love for her. Because of financial misfortunes, Emma finds herself unable to pay her large debts and pleads for Leon to help her, only to discover that he is a lowly office clerk. Rodolphe has returned from Italy, and, with the situation growing more and more urgent, she asks him to lend her money, but he refuses.  Knowing that all their property will be sold at auction, and that she will face shame and humiliation, she takes arsenic and dies a painful death in the arms of her husband, who finally understands the unhappiness his wife has suffered. He and his little daughter leave Yonville to begin a new life elsewhere.  Flaubert is acquitted.

**Review Summary:**

*Time* (August 15, 1949) thought *Madame Bovary* Jennifer Jones's best picture to date and that her performance was "hardly ever out of focus." She was praised for portraying Emma Bovary's "moods and caprices with sensitive dexterity."

*The New York Times* (August 26, 1949) complimented Jennifer Jones for her ability to wear the period costumes so beautifully, but thought her "a bit light" to accurately convey the "anguish of this classic dame."

**Other Sources:**
Reviews: *Christian Science Monitor*, November 18, 1949; *Commonweal*, September 2, 1949; *Cue*, August 27, 1949; *The Dallas Morning News*, September 17, 1949; *Film Daily*, August 1, 1949; *Hollywood Reporter*, August 1, 1949; *Life*, October 7, 1949; *Motion Picture Herald Product Digest*, August 6, 1949; *The New York Herald Tribune*, August 26, 1949; *The New York Journal of Commerce*, August 30, 1949; *The New Yorker*, September 3, 1949; *Newsweek*, August 29, 1949; *Rotarian*, November, 1949; *Theatre Arts*, November, 1949; *Variety*, August 3, 1949.
See Also: *Agee on Film*, Volume 1; *The Films of James Mason*; *The Novel and the Cinema*; *Novels Into Film*.

**Notes:**
*Madame Bovary* was only moderately successful at the box office, making 1949 a disappointing film year for Jennifer Jones.

F11   **CARRIE** (A Paramount Picture)

Released: June 11, 1952                 Running Time: 118 minutes

**Cast:**
Laurence Olivier (George Hurstwood); Jennifer Jones (Carrie Meeber); Miriam Hopkins (Julie Hurstwood); Eddie Albert (Charles Drouet); Basil Ruysdael (Mr. Fitzgerald); Ray Teal (Allan); Barry Kelley (Slawson); Sara Berner (Mrs. Oransky); William Regnolds (George Hurstwood, Jr.); Mary Murphy (Jessica Hurstwood); Harry Hayden (O'Brien); Charles Halton (Factory Foreman); Walter Baldwin (Carrie's Father); Dorothy Adams (Carrie's Mother); Jacqueline de Wit (Carrie's Sister); Harlan Briggs (Joe Brant); Melinda Plowman (Little Girl); Donald Kerr (Slawson's Bartender); Don Beddoe (Mr. Goodman); John Alvin (Stage manager).

**Credits:**
Director, Producer (William Wyler); Screenplay (Ruth and Augustus Goetz, from the novel by Theodore Dreiser), Photography (Victor Milner, ASC);

Music (David Raksin); Art Director (Hal Periera, Roland Anderson); Editor (Robert Swink); Costumes (Edith Head).

**Synopsis:**
In 1900, Carrie Meeber leaves her family in Missouri and takes a trian to Chicago. En route she meets Charlie Drouet, a self-assured traveling salesman who urges her to look him up sometime. She finds work in a sweatshop, but she loses the job, looks up Charlie to seek his assistance. He invites her to dinner at a restaurant managed by George Hurstwood. George begins courting Carrie, being careful not to tell her her of his unhappy marriage to Julie. Charlie eventually tells Carrie that her suitor is married, but she believes George when he says he will marry her as soon as he can secure a divorce. In a last-ditch attempt to find happiness, he steals $10,000 from his employer and takes Carrie with him to New York, where they pose as man and wife. His former employer sends a bondsman to find him, and fearing jail, George gives up what remains of the money and he and Carrie move into a cheap neighborhood. He manages to find work as a waiter, but he is soon fired, and matters are made worse by Carrie's pregnancy. Julie and her lawyer arrive and George, desperate for a divorce, signs away all claim to her property. Things get worse, and George is unable to find lasting work. When Carrie loses the baby, she leaves George and seeks work as an actress, eventually becoming a star. George, now a derelict, visits Carrie one night backstage and asks her for money and some food. She leaves to arrange for food to be brought in. Left alone, George considers suicide, but changes his mind, takes a quarter from Carrie's purse, and stumbles out of the theatre into the dark night.

**Review Summary:**
*The New York Times* (July 17, 1952) thought Laurence Olivier's portrait of Hurstwood was loyal to the book, but that Jones's portrayal of Carrie had nothing in common with Dreiser's heroine, terming it "coy." The reviewer said that her "soft seraphic portrait of Carrie" reduced the drama's theme to merely that of "hopeless, deathless love."

*The Hollywood Reporter* (June 9, 1952), however, considered Jennifer "perfect in the role" of Carrie, and that to leave audiences with the impresison that while others fall around her, Carrie will always survive, was "sheer artistry on her part."

**Other Sources:**
Reviews: *BFI Monthly Film Bulletin*, July, 1952; *Catholic World*, August, 1952; *Christian Century*, October 8, 1952; *Commonweal*, August 1, 1952; *Film Daily*, June 11, 1952; *Films in Review*, March, 1952; *Illustrated London News*, July 26, 1952; *Library Journal*, July, 1952; *The London Times*, July 7, 1952; *Motion Picture Herald Product Digest*, June 14, 1952; *The Nation*, May 17, 1952; *The New Statesman and Nation*, July 12, 1952; *The New Yorker*, July 26, 1952; *Newsweek*, July 28, 1952; *Saturday*

*Review*, July 12, 1952; *Sight and Sound*, July-September, 1952; *The Spectator*, July 4, 1952; *The Tatler*, July 16, 1952; *Time*, June 30, 1952; *Variety*, June 11, 1952.

See Also: *The Classic American Novel and the Movies*; *Film Comment*, Fall, 1980; *The Films of Laurence Olivier*; *Laurence Olivier* (Hirsch); *Laurence Olivier: Theatre and Cinema*; *Magills Survey of Cinema*, Series II; *William Wyler*; *A Guide to References and Resources*; *William Wyler* (Anderegg); *William Wyler* (Madsen).

**Notes:**
Two endings were filmed for *Carrie*: one had Hurstwood committing suicide by turning on the gas in Carrie's dressing room, and the other had him taking the coin and walking out into the night. The suicide ending was considered too grim, so the other ending was used, but audiences found it just as grim. The film was not a commercial success.

F12   **THE WILD HEART** (A Powell-Pressburger Production)

Released: May 29, 1952                      Running Time: 82 minutes

**Cast:**
Jennifer Jones (Hazel Woodus); David Farrar (Jack Reddin); Cyril Cusack (Edward Marston); Sybil Thorndike (Mrs. Marston); Edward Chapman (Mr. James); Esmond Knight (Abel Woodus); Hugh Griffith (Andrew Vessons); George Cole (Albert); Beatrice Varley (Aunt Prowde); Frances Clare (Amelia Comber); Raymond Rollett (Elder/Landlord); Gerald Lawson (Elder/Roadmender).

**Credits:**
Director, Producer, Screenplay (Michael Powell, Emeric Pressburger, from the novel by Mary Webb); Photographer (Chris Challis); Music (Brian Easdale); Art Director (Arthur Lawson); Film Editor (Reginald Mills); Technicolor Consultant (Joan Bridge).

**Synopsis:**
Hazel Woodus, a young woman who lives with her father in the wild country of Shropshire, is extremely superstitious, finding solace in the crude parables taught her by her gypsy mother. Her only friend is a half-tamed fox, named Foxy. She especially fears the Black Huntsman, a legendary phantom who rides the wild country and brings death to all who look upon him. Returning home one night after visiting relatives, she hears approaching hoofs, and runs, but it is Jack Reddin, who offers to give her a ride. Instead, he takes her to his home and tries to seduce her, but she runs away and is given shelter in the barn by Jack's stablemate, who takes her home the next morning. Her father decrees that she should marry, so she agrees to marry the first man to

ask her. It turns out to be Edward Marston, the local minister, and she marries him despite the opposition of Jack, who is still taken with the superstitious Hazel. Their marriage is not a happy one, however, with Edward refusing to share her bed, and she accepts Jack's offer to become his mistress. She is attracted to Jack, but fears his darker nature. She gives protection to a wounded rabbit, but when Jack allows his hound to to kill the animal, Hazel vows she will also die young. Edward comes to get Hazel, even though she is carrying Jack's child. She and Edward seem to find brief happiness but the church elders demand that Hazel be sent away because of her adulterous affair with Jack. Edward proposes that they go away to start a new life, but before his plans can be realized, Hazel wanders away in search of her lost pet, Foxy. She is startled by hunters' dogs, and falls into an open mine pit, dying young just as she had predicted.

**Review Summary**:
*Variety* (September 27, 1952) thought Jennifer Jones's performance as Hazel Woodus "genuine and at times glowing."

*The Hollywood Reporter* (May 28, 1952) thought her role difficult, but said she handled it with "great beauty and skill," and termed her performance "arresting."

**Other Sources**:
Reviews: *Commonweal*, June 20, 1952; *Film Daily*, May 29, 1952; *Library Journal*, June 15, 1952; *Motion Picture Herald Product Digest*, May 31, 1952; *National Parent-Teacher*, September, 1952; *The New York Times*, May 29, 1952; *Newsweek*, June 9, 1952; *Saturday Review*, June 28, 1952; *Sequence*, New Year 1951; *Time,* June 9, 1952.

**Notes**:
*The Wild Heart* was first released in England in late 1950 under its original title *Gone to Earth*, but reviews were poor and Selznick, who owned the North American distribution rights, edited the film and changed its title before releasing it to American theatres. American reviews were no better, although most critics were kind to Jennifer.

F13    **RUBY GENTRY** (A Bernhard-Vidor Production)

Released: December 29, 1952                    Running Time: 82 minutes

**Cast**:
Jennifer Jones (Ruby Gentry); Charlton Heston (Boake Tackman); Karl Malden (Jim Gentry); Tom Tully (Jud Corey); Bernard Phillips (Dr. Saul Manfred); James Anderson (Jewel Corey); Josephine Hutchinson (Letitia Gentry); Phyllis Avery (Tracy MacAuliffe); Herbert Heyes (Judge

Tackman); Myra Marsh (Ma Corey); Charles Kane (Cullen MacAuliffe); Sam Flint (Neil Fallgren); Frank Wilcox (Clyde Pratt).

**Credits**:
Director (King Vidor); Producers (Joseph Bernhard, King Vidor); Screenplay (Sylvia Richards); Photographer (Russell Harlan, ASC); Music (Heinz Roemheld); Film Editor (Terry Morie); Art Director (Dan Hall); Music Supervision (David Chudnow).

**Synopsis**:
In the backwoods town of Braddock, North Carolina, Ruby Corey was from the wrong side of the tracks, but was scheming to get ahead. She falls in love with Boake Tackman, just back from South America with an ambitious plan to turn his family plantation into a modern truck farm. Ruby, despite the warnings of her brother that Boake will not marry beneath him, has an open affair with the man, but Boake announces his plans to marry a local girl of social standing. Ruby is furious, but she finds herself being proposed to by Jim Gentry, the town's richest man. They are married, but the townspeople do not accept her. She meets Boake at a country club dance and her open attentions toward him anger Jim who calls her a tramp. The next day, Jim takes Ruby sailing, but he is drowned in an accident, and it is Ruby who is blamed by the townspeople. To seek revenge, she uses her position as the widow of the town's richest man to forclose on everyone who had outstanding debts to her husband, resulting in the closing of factories and even the local newspaper. She tells Boake she could ruin him too, if she wanted to, and makes him a generous offer, but he merely scoffs at her. She takes control of his plantation, topples the signs, and has a hole cut in the dyke, allowing the sea to rush in and reclaim the land. Later, when Boake and Ruby join a group of duckhunters, they are stalked by Ruby's brother, a religious zealot who demands that she be punished for her evil deeds. He kills Boake, and Ruby responds by coolly shooting her brother and hiding his body in the swamp. The years pass, but Ruby has become a bitter, fishing boat skipper, unable to rise above her lowly background.

**Review Summary**:
The *Hollywood Reporter* (December 23, 1952) was conservative in its review, merely saying that Jennifer Jones "effectively gallops the full gamut of emotions" required by the role.

*Newsweek* (January 12, 1953) was not impressed, calling the film a "very improbable and sadly conceived" vehicle for Miss Jones.

**Additional Sources**:
Reviews: *BFI Monthly Film Bulletin*, March, 1953; *Cue*, December 27, 1952; *Film Daily*, December 29, 1952; *The London Times*, January 19, 1953; *Motion Picture Herald Product Digest*, December 27, 1952; *National Parent-Teacher*, January, 1953; *The New Statesman and Nation*, January 24,

1953; *The New York Times*, December 26, 1952; *Variety*, December 24, 1952.
See Also: *Film Comment*, September/October, 1973; *The Films of Charlton Heston*; *Selected Film Criticism 1951-60*.

**Notes:**
*Ruby Gentry* was the first box office hit for Jenifer Jones in six years, and it helped to re-establish her questionable standing. King Vidor had also directed Jones in *Duel in the Sun*, and he later said that he understood how to direct the actress better than most directors. To his credit, "Pearl Chavez" and "Ruby Gentry" are two of Jennifer's best portrayals. One scene required Jones to strike Heston on the jaw, and she played the scene with such vigor that her hand was broken.

F14    **INDISCRETION OF AN AMERICAN WIFE**    (A Selznick Production)

Released: July 1954                              Running Time: 63 minutes

**Cast:**
Jennifer Jones (Mary); Montgomery Clift (Giovanni); Gino Cervi (Commissioner); Richard Beymer (Paul).

**Credits:**
Director, Producer (Vittorio De Sica); Dialogue (Truman Capote); Art Director (Virgilio Marchi); Screenplay (Cesare Zavattini, Luigi Chiarini, Giorgio Prosperi); Photography (G.R. Aldo); Music (Alessandro Cicognini); Costumes (Christian Dior).

**Synopsis:**
Mary Forbes, a Philadelphia housewife vacationing in Rome, arrives at Rome's Terminal Station and inquires about the next train to Milano. She has decided that her husband and daughter back in the states are more important than Giovanni, the Italian man with whom she has been having an affair. She phones her nephew, asking him to bring her bags to the station and then buys a gift for her daughter. She boards the train, but sees Gionvanni on the platform and, acting on impulse, leaves the train and greets him. They sit in a restaurant where he asks her to remain in Italy with him, but she tells him she must return to her family. She does, however, accept his offer to return to his apartment, but she sees her nephew hurrying with her luggage. She urges the boy to return home, but he lingers and sees Giovanni slap Mary when she decides not to go to his flat after all. Giovanni leaves and Mary and the boy wait for the later train to leave. She helps an ill pregnant woman, buys candy for her children, and sends Paul away. Meanwhile, Giovanni has cooled down and has returned to the station in search of Mary. She spies him across

the tracks, and he hurries toward her and is almost struck by an on-coming train. They enter a deserted coach, but are spotted by a train policeman and taken to the commissioner. She tells the commissioner that she plans to take the 8:30 train to Paris, leaving Giovanni and her memories behind He tears up the complaint. Only ten minutes remain until the train leaves, so Giovanni helps her aboard, but they are unable to kiss, and Giovanni stumbles onto the track as the train pulls away.

**Review Summary**:
*The New York Times* (June 26, 1954) cared little for the film, but thought Jennifer portrayed the troubled woman with "dignity and sentiment."

*The Hollywood Reporter* (April 21, 1954) found the story of little interest, but admitted that the "beautifully sensitive performances" of Jones and Clift almost saved it from mediocrity.

**Additional Sources**:
Reviews: *American*, July 17, 1954; *BFI Monthly Film Bulletin*, September, 1954; *Catholic World*, May, 1954; *Commonweal*, May 7, 1954; *Coronet*, May, 1954; *Farm Journal*, July, 1954; *Film Daily,* April 30, 1954; *Films and Filming*, October, 1954; *Films in Review*, April, 1954; *The London Times*, August 5, 1954; *Motion Picture Herald Product Digest*, April 24, 1954; *National Parent-Teacher*, April, 1954; *The New Statesman and Nation*, August 14, 1954; *Newsweek*, April 12, 1954; *Saturday Review*, April 24, 1954; *Sight and Sound*, October/December, 1954; *Time*, April 26, 1954; *Variety*, April 21, 1954.
See Also: *The Films of Montgomery Clift*.

**Notes**:
Originally titled *Terminal Station*, the film was first released in Europe, where it ran close to two hours, and although reviewers were kind, Selznick heavily edited the film and changed the title before distributing it in America where critics disliked the film and audiences weren't interested.

F15 **BEAT THE DEVIL** (A United Artists Production)

Released: March 3, 1954                    Running Time: 92 minutes
**Cast**:
Humphrey Bogart (Billy Dannreuther); Jennifer Jones (Gwendolyn Chelm); Gina Lollobrigida (Maria Dannreuther); Robert Morley (Petersen); Peter Lorre (O'Hara); Edward Underdown (Harry Chelm); Ivor Barnard (Major Ross); Marco Tulli (Ravello); Bernard Lee (CID Inspector); Mario Perroni (Purser); Alex Pochet (Hotel Manager); Aldo Silvani (Charles); Giulio Donni (Administrator); Mimo Poli (Barman); Manuel Serano (Arab Officer); Saro Urzi (Captain); Juan de Landa (Hispano-Suiza Driver).

**Credits:**
Director (John Huston); Associate Producer (Jack Clayton); Screenplay (Truman Capote, John Huston, from the novel by James Helvick); Photography (Oswald Morris, BSC); Music (Franco Mannino); Editor (Ralph Kemplen).

**Synopsis:**
In an Italian seaport, Billy and Maria Dannreuther join forces with a motley crew of fortune hunters in a plan to get to British East Africa to claim a piece of uranium rich land. The group has to wait, however, until the ship captain sobers up enough to take them there, but he's in no hurry. Waiting for the same vessel are Harry and Gwendolyn Chelm. Billy and Maria take the Chelms on a scenic motor ride and Gwendolyn tells Billy she and her husband are going to Africa because the land is teeming with uranium, but Billy recognizes her as a compulsive liar. Finally, the captain is sober, and the group begins their voyage to Africa. One of Billy's friends runs a check on the Chelms and finds out that they are nobodies, but Maria nonetheless falls for Harry, and Gwendolyn makes an obvious play for Billy. The ship's power fails, and although Harry tries to fix the engine, it explodes, and the group (sans Harry) must travel the remaining distance to Africa in a lifeboat, but are captured upon arriving by Arab tribesmen. They manage to escape and get to the African port where they had originally planned to dock. Harry is presumed dead, but a sudden cable arrives for Gwendolyn from Harry. He tells her that he is not only alive, but has acquired control of the African uranium market and urges her to join him.

**Review Summary:**
*Time* (March 8, 1954) thought Jennifer Jones outstanding, managing "to catch the mystic fervor of the truly creative liar."

*The New York Times* (March 13, 1954) thought Jennifer Jones was "luscious and talented."

**Additional Sources:**
Reviews: *BFI Monthly Film Bulletin*, January, 1954; *Catholic World*, April, 1954; *Commonweal*, March 19, 1954; *Coronet*, April, 1954; *Farm Journal*, May, 1954; *Film Daily*, March 3, 1954; *Films in Review*, March, 1954; *Hollywood Reporter*, March 2, 1954; *Library Journal*, March 1, 1954; *Look*, September 22, 1953; *Motion Picture Herald Product Digest*, March 6, 1954; *National Parent-Teacher*, April, 1954; *The New Statesman and Nation*, December 5, 1953; *The New York Herald Tribune*, March 13, 1954; *The New York Times Magazine*, September 27, 1953; *Newsweek*, March 8, 1954; *Punch*, December 9, 1953; *Saturday Review*, March 13, 1954; *Senior Scholastic*, March 10, 1954; *Sight and Sound*, January-March, 1954; *Variety*, December 22, 1953.
See Also: *American Film*, September, 1980; *The Cinema of John Huston*; *Cinema, the Magic Vehicle*; *The Complete Films of Humphrey Bogart*; *Film*

*Society Review*, January, 1966; *The Films of John Huston*; *The Films of Gina Lollobrigida*; *The Films of Peter Lorre*; *Humphrey Bogart, the Man and His Films*; *John Huston* (Hammen); *Kiss Kiss Bang Bang*; *Magills Survey of Cinema*, Series II; *Movie Comedy* (Byron); *The New York Post*, March 5, 1988.

**Notes:**
Gwendolen Chelm was the second and last comic character Jennifer Jones portrayed. She revealed a nice sense of timing perfectly suited for comedies and it is a pity she was never allowed to develop this side of her persona.


F16    **LOVE IS A MANY-SPLENDORED THING** (A 20th Century-Fox Production)

Released: August 10, 1955                    Running Time: 102 minutes

**Cast:**
William Holden (Mark Elliott); Jennifer Jones (Dr. Han Suyin); Torin Thatcher (Mr. Palmer-Jones); Isobel Elsom (Adeline Palmer-Jones); Murray Matheson (Dr. Tam); Virginia Gregg (Ann Richards); Richard Loo (Robert Hung); Soo Yong (Nora Hung); Philip Ahn (Third Uncle); Jorja Curtright (Suzanne); Candace Lee (Oh-No); Donna Martell (Suchen); Kam Tong (Dr. Sen); James Hong (Fifth Brother); Herbert Heyes (Father Low); Angela Loo (Mei Loo); Marie Tsien (Rosie Wu); Eleanor Moore (English Secretary); Barbara Jean Wong, Hazel Shon (Nurses); Kei Chung (Interne).

**Credits:**
Director (Henry King); Producer (Buddy Adler); Screenplay (John Patrick, from the novel by Han Suyin); Photography (Leon Shamroy, ASC); Music (Alfred Nerman); Film Editor (William Reynolds, ACE).

**Synopsis:**
At the Victoria Hospital in Hong Kong, Dr. Han Suyin, a Eurasian, is popular with her patients and co-workers alike. Since the death of her husband at the hands of the Communists, she has had little interest in a social life, but when she meets Mark, a foreign correspondent, there is an immediate attraction between them. They begin a relationship, although Dr. Suyin resists at first, feeling that she must remain dedicated to her work. They meet on a hill behind the hospital and Mark confesses his love for her and his desire to marry her, but a family crisis in China forces Dr. Suyin to leave. She tells Mark that her Eurasian background will only cause them trouble. In China, Dr. Suyin learns that the Communists are trying to take over the region where her family live. Mark, who has followed her to China, asks her again to marry him. Her family grant their permission, although reluntantly, but Mark is already married and his wife refuses to give him a divorce. They

share a wonderful week in Macao together before Mark is suddenly called to Korea on an important mission. While he is gone, Dr. Suyin's residency at the hospital is terminated and she is forced to search for work. Without warning, Mark is killed by a bomb explosion in Korea, and Dr. Suyin returns to the hill and imagines she sees him.

**Review Summary:**
*Variety* (August 10, 1955) found Jennifer Jones a "pure delight" as Han Suyin. Her performance was described as "remarkable," completely capturing the spirit of the book.

*The New York Times* (August 19, 1955) thought she was "lovely and intense," and her beauty was said to reflect both "sunshine and sadness."

**Additional Sources:**
<u>Reviews</u>: *American*, August 27, 1955; *BFI Monthly Film Bulletin*, November, 1955; *Catholic World*, October, 1955; *Commonweal*, September 9, 1955; *Film Daily*, August 10, 1955; *Films and Filming*, November, 1955; *Hollywood Reporter*, August 10, 1955; *Library Journal*, October 1, 1955; *The New Yorker*, August 27, 1955; *Newsweek*, August 29, 1955; *Time*, September 12, 1955.
<u>See Also</u>: *The Films of William Holden*; *Magills Survey of Cinema*, Series II.

**Notes:**
For her performance as Dr. Han Suyin, Jennifer Jones received her fifth and last Academy Award nomination to date. She lost the Oscar to Anna Magnani.


F17    **GOOD MORNING, MISS DOVE**    (A 20th Century-Fox Production)

Released: November 22, 1955                    Running Time: 107 minutes

**Cast:**
Jennifer Jones (Miss Dove); Robert Stack (Tom Baker); Kipp Hamilton (Jincey Baker); Robert Douglas (Mr. Porter); Peggy Knudsen (Billie Jean); Marshall Thompson (Mr. Pendleton); Chuck Connors (Bill Holloway); Biff Elliott (Rev. Alex Burnham); Jerry Paris (Maurice); Mary Wickes (Miss Ellwood); Ted Marc (David Burnham); Dick Stewart (Dr. Temple); Vivian Marshall (Mrs. Meggs); Richard Deacon (Mr. Spivey); Bill Walker (Henry); Than Wyenn (Mr. Levine); Leslie Bradley (Alonso Dove); Robert Lynn, Sr. (Dr. Hurley); Edward Firestone (Fred Makepeace); Martha Wentworth (Grandma Holloway); Virginia Christine (Mrs. Rigsbee); Cheryl Callaway (Annabel); Mark Engel (Marksie); Mae Marsh (Woman in Bank).

**Credits:**
Director (Henry Koster); Producer (Samuel G. Engel); Screenplay (Eleanore Griffin, from the novel by Frances Gray Patton); Photography (Leon Shamroy, ASC); Music (Leigh Harline); Art Direction (Lyle Wheeler, Mark-Lee Kirk); Film Editor (William Reynolds, ACE); Special Effects (Ray Kellogg).

**Synopsis:**
In the town of Liberty Hall, Miss Dove is a well-known and highly respected teacher, a strict teacher who rules her classroom with an iron hand. She is suddenly stricken in the classroom by a sharp pain in her lower spine, and has the doctor father of one of her pupils come to attend her. Her thoughts go back to when she was a young woman in love and with a bright future, a woman with no desire to become a schoolteacher. Suddenly her father dies, leaving behind an enormous debt. She takes a job teaching school to pay back the debt, and sends her suitor away. Her thoughts suddenly return to the present and she finds herself being carried to the hospital, where she is cared for by a former pupil who talks continually about the town policeman, another former pupil, who, under Miss Dove's guidance, had overcome a poverty-stricken background. In her hospital room, Miss Dove is visited by two other former pupils, one a now-successful playwright and the other a prisoner in the town's jail. She learns that an operation must be performed to remove a growth on her spine, and when the surgery begins, two other former students stand by, ready to donate blood. The school's principal dismisses classes so the students can await news of the operation's outcome. It is a success, and Miss Dove is touched by the crowd who has gathered under her window to wish her well, but in typical fashion, she sends instructions for her students to begin studying for the upcoming geography examination.

**Review Summary:**
*Variety* (November 16, 1955) thought the performance of Jennifer Jones was "moving" and "throat-catching."

*The New York Times* (November 24, 1955) was equally impressed, describing her portrait of the prim school teacher as being "carefully etched," with a "neat blend of pride, genuine gentility and humor."

**Additional Sources:**
Reviews: *America*, December 10, 1955; *Catholic World*, January, 1956; *Commonweal*, December 9, 1955; *Films in Review*, December, 1955; *Library Journal*, December 15, 1955; *Motion Picture Herald Product Digest*, November 19, 1955; *The New Yorker*, December 3, 1955; *Newsweek*, December 5, 1955; *Time*, December 5, 1955.

**Notes:**
Mae Marsh (woman in bank) had been an important star for D.W. Griffith.

## F18    THE MAN IN THE GRAY FLANNEL SUIT (A 20th Century-Fox Production)

Released: March 30, 1956                    Running Time: 153 minutes

**Cast:**
Gregory Peck (Tom Rath); Jennifer Jones (Betsy Rath); Fredric March (Hopkins); Marisa Pavan (Maria); Lee J. Cobb (Judge Bernstein); Ann Harding (Mrs. Hopkins); Keenan Wynn (Caesar Gardell); Gene Lockhart (Hawthorne); Gigi Perreau (Susan Hopkins); Portland Mason (Janie); Arthur O'Connell (Walker); Henry Daniell (Bill Ogden); Connie Gilchrist (Mrs. Manter); Joseph Sweeney (Edward Schultz); Sandy Descher (Barbara); Mickey Maga (Pete); Kenneth Tobey (Mahoney); Ruth Clifford (Florence); Geraldine Wall (Miriam); Alex Campbell (Johnson); Jerry Hall (Freddie); Jack Mather (Police Sergeant); Frank Wilcox (Dr. Pearce); Nan Martin (Miss Lawrence); Tris Coffin (Byron Holgate); William Phillips (Bugala); Leon Alton (Cliff); De Forrest Kelley (Medic).

**Credits:**
Director (Nunnally Johnson); Producer (Darryl F. Zanuck); Screenplay (Nunnally Johnson, from the novel by Sloan Wilson); Photography (Charles G. Clarke, ASC); Music (Bernard Herrmann); Art Direction (Lyle R. Wheeler, Jack Martin Smith); Film Editor (Dorothy Spencer); Special Effects (Ray Kellogg, ASC).

**Synopsis:**
Tom and Betsy Rath are typical suburbanites. He commutes from their home in Connecticut to a job in New York that pays a salary barely enabling him to support his wife and three children. His wife has lost faith in him and pressures him to better himself and to get a better house. A man with a checkered war past, Tom sets himself up for an interview with a new public relations firm. While writing his biography as part of the application, he remembers his tragic war experiences and thinks he will be passed over for the job, but he is hired. His first assignment is to ghost-write a speech but he is taken off the project when he disagrees with the subject. The head of the firm has taken a liking to Tom because of his sound judgement and honesty. Meanwhile, Betsy has sold their home in Connecticut and moved the family into an outdated old mansion. Through an unusual circumstance, Tom learns that a girl in Italy bore his illigitimate son, and wants him to support the child. When he tells Betsy about his Italian child, she reacts violently, but eventually comes around and agrees to send money to the child's mother. He is offered a more challenging job at the firm, but he turns it down, saying his first responsibility is to his wife and family.

**Review Summary:**
*Films in Review* (May, 1956) thought Jennifer "too neurotic for the wholesome Betsy Rath," and scolded her for "misconceiving the role."

*Variety*  (April 4, 1956)was equally critical, and thought Jennifer showed "no feeling of any real relationship" toward Peck, although the script called for her to do so.

**Additional Sources:**
Reviews: *Cue*, April 14, 1956; *Film Daily*, March 30, 1956; *Life*, November 7, 1955, April 9, 1956; *Look*, May 15, 1956; *The New York Herald Tribune*, April 13, 1956; *The New York Times*, April 13, 1956; *New Yorker*, April 21, 1957; *Saturday Review*, April 21, 1956.
See Also: *The Films of Fredric March*; *The Films of Gregory Peck*.

**Notes:**
*The Man in the Gray Flannel Suit* was the third and final film for Jones as part of her 1955, three-picture deal with 20th Century-Fox. It was also her second and last film with Gregory Peck.

F19    **THE BARRETTS OF WIMPOLE STREET** (A Metro-Goldwyn-Mayer Production)

Released: February 1, 1957                    Running Time: 106 minutes

**Cast:**
Jennifer Jones (Elizabeth); John Gielgud (Barrett); Bill Travers (Robert Browning); Virginia McKenna (Henrietta); Susan Stephen (Bella); Vernon Gray (Capt. Surtees Cook); Jean Anderson (Wilson); Maxine Audley (Arabel); Leslie Phillips (Harry Bevan); Laurence Naismith (Dr. Chambers); Moultrie Kelsall (Dr. Ford-Waterlow); Michael Brill (George); Kenneth Fortiscue (Octavius); Nicholas Hawtrey (Henry); Richard Thorp (Alfred); Keith Baxter (Charles); Brian Smith (Septimus).

**Credits:**
Director (Sidney Franklin); Producer (Sam Zimbalist); Screenplay (John Dighton, from the play by Rudolf Besier); Film Editor (Frank Clarke); Music (Bronislau Kaper); Art Director (Alfred Junge, FBKS); Camera Operator (John Harris); Continuity (Hazel Swift).

**Synopsis:**
In London, at 50 Wimpole Street, live the Barretts, stern Edward Barrett and his nine children, whom he rules with an iron hand. He is especially protective of his semi-invalid daughter, Elizabeth, whom he prohibits from leaving the house. She spends her time reading poetry, and when she is puzzled by a poem of Robert Browning, she writes to him. Expecting a written reply, she is shocked when the poet calls in person. She is immediately attracted by his enthusiasm for life, love and art. Browning visits again, which enrages Elizabeth's father, and when she asks permission

to spend some time in Italy where she believes her health will improve, he refuses, and prohibits her from receiving any other visitors. She does happen to meet Browning again, and he proclaims his love for her in the botanical gardens. Mr. Barrett, sensing that he is losing control of his daughter, decides to move the entire family to the country where his control will be complete. Browning, however, proposes an immediate marriage, which Elizabeth accepts. She sneaks out of the house as Mr. Barrett is blessing the evening meal, and when he discovers that his daughter has defied him, he tries to bring her back, but is too late; she has already become Mrs. Robert Browning. The couple travel to Italy where their love poetry will bring them world-wide fame.

**Review Summary:**
*The New York Herald Tribune* (January 13, 1957) couldn't accept Jennifer Jones as the "ethereal type," and found it hard to believe that she could write sensitive poetry.

*Variety* (January 16, 1957) thought Jennifer a "surprisingly healthy-looking Elizabeth" but admitted her handling of the role was skillful.

**Additional Sources:**
Reviews: *Christian Science Monitor*, January 29, 1957; *Cue*, January 19, 1957; *Film Daily*, January 8, 1957; *London Observer*, March 3, 1957; *The New York Sunday News*, December 23, 1956; *The New York Times*, January 18, 1957; *New Yorker*, January 26, 1957; *Saturday Review*, January 26, 1957.

**Notes:**
*The Barretts of Wimpole Street* was a resounding success for all concerned, especially for director Sidney Franklin, who had directed the same story in 1934 with Norma Shearer as the poetess and Fredric March as Robert Browning.


F20   **A FAREWELL TO ARMS**   (A 20th Century-Fox Production)

Released: December, 1957                    Running Time: 152 minutes
**Cast:**
Rock Hudson (Lt. Frederick Henry); Jennifer Jones (Nurse Catherine Barkley); Vittorio De Sica (Maj. Alessandro Rinaldi); Oscar Homolka (Dr. Emerich); Mercedes McCambridge (Miss Van Campen); Elaine Stritch (Helen Ferguson); Kurt Kasznar (Bonello); Victor Francen (Col. Valentini); Franco Interlenghi (Aymo); Leopoldo Trieste (Passini); Jose Nieto (Major Stampi); Georges Brehat (Captain Bassi); Johanna Hofer (Mrs. Zimmerman); Eduard Linkers (Lt. Zimmerman); Umberto Sacripanti

(Ambulance Driver); Joan Shawlee (Nurse); Memmo Carotennto (Nino); Alberto Sordi (Father Galli).

## Credits:
Director (Charles Vidor); Producer (David O. Selznick); Screenplay (Ben Hecht, based on the novel by Ernest Hemingway); Photography (Piero Portalupi, AIC, Oswald Morris, BSC); Music (Mario Nascimbene); Art Direction (Mario Garbuglia); Production Design (Alfred Junge); Film Editors (James E. Newcom, Gerald J. Wilson, John M. Foley, ACE).

## Synopsis:
In Italy during World War I, Lt. Frederick Henry, meets nurse Catherine Barkley before returning to the front. They make love in a deserted summer house while seeking shelter from a sudden rain storm, and the next morning, she pushes through the crowds to see him off. Lt. Henry is wounded in battle and Nurse Barkley asks to be transferred to the hospital in which he is a patient. There they continue their romance under the watchful eye of head nurse Miss Van Campen. As Frederick improves, Catherine confesses that she is pregnant and Frederick suggests an immediate marriage, but she refuses. Nurse Van Campen learns of their romance and orders that Lt. Henry be sent back to the front. The war escalates and he and his friend Major Rinaldi are captured and sentenced to death as German spies. Rinaldi is executed, but Frederick escapes and returns to Catherine. Fearing for their safety, they escape across a lake into Switzerland where they find shelter in a small hotel and await the birth of their baby. Catherine's labor is difficult, and the infant, a boy, is stillborn. Catherine is predicted to recover, but a sudden hemorrhage kills her, and Frederick realizes that his farewell to arms has become shockingly real.

## Review Summary:
*The New York Times* (January 25, 1958) thought Jennifer Jones portrayed Catherine Barkley with "bewildering nervous moves and grimmaces," and said the love between the nurse and the soldier was "intensely acted, not realized."

*Variety* (December 25, 1957) said Jennifer "only sporadically rises to the full challenge" of the difficult role, and lamented that, in the hands of Miss Jones, the nurse "frequently lacks warmth."

## Additional Sources:
Reviews: *America*, January 25, 1958; *BFI Monthly Film Bulletin*, May, 1958; *Commonweal*, February 7, 1958; *Film Daily*, December 19, 1957, April, 1958; *Films and Filming*, April, 1958; *Films in Review*, January, 1958; *Hollywood Reporter*, December 19, 1957; *The London Observer*, March 30, 1958; *The London Times*, March 30, 1958; *Motion Picture Herald Product Digest*, December 21, 1957; *The New Republic*, February 17, 1958; *The New Yorker*, February 1, 1958; *Newsweek*, December 30, 1957; *Saturday Review*, February 1, 1958; *Time*, Febryary 3, 1958.

See Also: *Christian Science Monitor*, April 16, 1957; *The Classic American Novel and the Cinema*; *Hemingway on Film*; *Variety*, October 30, 1957.

**Notes:**
The failure of *A Farewell to Arms* ended Selznick's career as a producer, and put Jones off the screen for three years.


F21    **TENDER IS THE NIGHT** (A 20th Century-Fox Production)

Released: February 1, 1962                     Running Time: 146 minutes

**Cast:**
Jennifer Jones (Nicole Diver); Jason Robards (Dick Diver); Joan Fontaine (Baby Warren); Tom Ewell (Abe North); Cesare Danova (Tommy Barban); Jill St. John (Rosemary Hoyt); Paul Lukas (Dr. Dohmler); Bea Benaderet (Mrs. McKisco); Charles Fredericks (Mr. McKisco); Sanford Meisner (Dr. Gregorovious); Mac McWhorter (Colis Clay); Albert Carrier (Louis); Richard de Combray (Francisco); Carole Matthews (Mrs. Hoyt); Alan Napier (Pardo); Leslie Farrell (Topsy Diver); Michael Crisalli (Lanier Diver); Earl Grant (Piano Player); Maurice Dallimore (Sir Charles Golding); Carol Veazie (Mrs. Dunphrey); Vera de Winter (Nurse).

**Credits:**
Director (Henry King); Producer (Henry T. Weinstein); Screenplay (Ivan Moffat, from novel by F. Scott Fitzgerald); Photography (Leon Shamroy, ASC); Film Editor (William Reynolds, ACE); Music (Bernard Herrmann).

**Synopsis:**
The wealthy Dick Divers give a 4th of July party, inviting all their American friends, and Nicole tries to act relaxed, but she is upset by her husband's attentions to a younger woman and the party ends when she screams her rage at him. The next morning, Dick remembers meeting Nicole at a Zurich sanitarium, where he had treated her for a nervous disorder. She recovers and they meet weeks later and she invites Dick to dine with her. Nicole's sister, Baby, suggests that Dick marry Nicole. He declines, but later realizes that he cannot let her out of his life. They marry and travel through Europe, but avoid Zurich. His thoughts return to the present and he informs Nicole that he is returning to Zurich. He does, learns that the sanitarium is under new management, and is persuaded to ask his wife to help him invest $200,000 in the sanitarium. He later meets his wife and daugher in Paris, and through some unfortunate circumstances, begins to lose his confidence. Dick and Nicole return to Zurich and invest the money. Dick returns to work, but he does not get along well with his patients, and Nicole suggests they go to the French Riviera where he can open a sanitarium of his own. But his confidence and self-respect are gone, and Nicole asks for a divorce. It is

granted and Dick heads for Glen Falls, New York, where he hopes to pick up the pieces of his professional life.

**Review Summary:**
*Variety* (January 17, 1962), thought Jennifer a "crisply fresh, intriguing personality" and termed her Nicole Diver a "striking character."

According to *Time* (January 26, 1962),Jennifer Jones overcame the problem of age and neurotic lip-twisting, and "does her best work in a decade."

**Additional Sources:**
Reviews: *Cue*, January 27, 1962; *Film Daily*, January 1, 1962; *Film Quarterly*, Spring, 1962; *Films and Filming*, April, 1962; *The London Sunday Times*, February 11, 1962; *The New York Herald Tribune*, January 20, 1962; *The New York Post*, January 21, 1962; *The New York Times*, January 20, 1962; *Observer*, February 11, 1962; *Saturday Review*, January 27, 1962.
See Also: *Variety*, May 31, 1961, August 30, 1961.

**Notes:**
Selznick had long intended to film Fitzgerald's novel, but it was 20th Century-Fox who brought the story to the screen, after Selznick sold them the rights.

F22    **THE IDOL** (An Embassy Production)

Released: August 1, 1966                    Running Time: 107 minutes

**Cast:**
Jennifer Jones (Carol); Michael Parks (Marco); John Leyton (Timothy); Jennifer Hilary (Sarah); Guy Doleman (Martin Livesay); Natasha Pyne (Rosalind); Jeremy Bulloch (Lewis); Fanny Carby (Barmaid); Caroline Blakiston (Second Woman at Party); Vernon Dobtcheff (Man at Party); Michael Gordon (Boy); Gordon Gostelow (Simon); Ken Haward (Policeman); Renee Houston (Woman at Party); Priscilla Morgan (Rosie); Edna Morris (Mrs. Muller); Peter Porteous (Tommy); Terry Richards, Derek Ware (Laborers); Jack Watson (Police Inspector); Rita Webb (Landlady); Tina Williams (Dorothea).

**Credits:**
Director (Daniel Petrie); Producer (Leonard Lightstone); Screenplay (Millard Lampell); Photography (Ken Higgins, BSC); Art Direction (George Provis); Editor (Jack Slade); Music (John Dankworth).

**Synopsis:**

Marco and Sarah, struggling art students, are introduced to Carol, the mother of their friend Timothy. Carol insists that her son pursue an education in medicine although he too would rather be a struggling art student. Marco tells Timothy that he is completely dominated by his mother, and he begins to realize that is indeed true. At a weekend party, Carol invites Marco, and Tim is dismayed to see Marco flirting with his mother. Several days later, Tim decides to live his own life, which means moving away from home and switching to an art course at school. Carol later invites Marco and his girlfriend, Sarah, to her country cottage for a house-warming, but is rather cool to Marco. Time passes, and on New Years Eve, Marco and Carol meet and Carol confesses that she was wrong in trying to dominate her son and that she doubts her ability to really be a woman. Marco responds by seducing her. Meanwhile Tim and Sarah are drawn to each other, and later, when Tim realizes what has happened between Marco and his mother, he and his friend go out alone on a barge. Marco commits suicide and Tim is arrested for murder. Tim refuses to tell the whole story, not wanting to drag his mother into the sordid affair, and is led away by the police.

**Review Summary**:
*The New York Times* (August 11, 1966) were extremely critical of the film, but thought Jennifer Jones gave a "workmanlike" performance.

*The New York Morning Telegraph* (August 11, 1966) thought Jennifer Jones still had "certain traces" of the charm and talent that had first made her a star, but considered the choice for a film vehicle "lamentable."

**Additional Sources**:
Reviews: *America*, September 3, 1966; *BFI Monthly Film Bulletin*, November, 1966; *Christian Science Monitor* (Western Edition), January 6, 1967; *Film Daily*, August 3, 1966; *Filmfacts*, October 15, 1966; *Films and Filming*, December, 1966; *Life*, September 16, 1966; *The London Observer*, October 9, 1966; *The London Times*, October 6, 1966; *New Statesman*, October 7, 1966; *Time*, August 19, 1966; *Variety*, August 3, 1966.
See Also: *Warner-Pathe News*, October 3, 1966.

**Notes**:
Jennifer Jones was a last-minute replacement for Kim Stanley, who withdrew from the project due to illness. Interviewed while on location, she said she had been the original choice, but had turned down the offer.

F23  **ANGEL, ANGEL, DOWN WE GO** (An American International Pictures Production)

Released: August, 1969                    Running Time: 93 minutes

**Cast:**
Jennifer Jones (Astrid); Jordan Christopher (Bogart); Roddy McDowall
(Santoro); Holly Near (Tara Nicole); Lou Rawls (Joe); Charles Aidman
(Willy); Davey Davison (Anna Livia); Marty Brill (Maitre D').

**Credits:**
Director (Robert Thom); Producer (Jerome F. Katzman); Executive
Producer (Sam Katzman); Screenplay (Robert Thom); Photography (Jack
Warren); Film Editor (Eve Newman); Art Director (Gabriel Scognamillo);
Choreographer (Wilda Taylor).

**Synopsis:**
Tara Nicole remembers that she had always thought her wealthy parents
were perfect, but was aware that they sometimes quarrelled, even remembers
seeing her father in the shower with a young man. Following a bitter
argument, the girl was sent to a school in Switzerland. Several years later,
Tara, now 18, returns home and her mother plans an elaborate coming-out
party for her daughter, but she wanders through the crowd of people, not
quite fitting into the wild spirit of the party. After the party she meets
Bogart, who was the head of a band her mother had engaged for the party,
and they begin a love-making spree that lasts several days. Tara feels accepted. The girl's parents wonder where their child is, but soon find out when
the wandering melange of young people, of which Tara is now a member,
arrive at their home and virtually take over. Bogart seduces Astrid and Tara
becomes aware of the relationship between them. They take-up sky diving,
and Astrid joins in their fun, though she has a terrible fear of flying. As her
husband, recently returned from a business trip, watches, Astrid is unable to
open her chute and plunges to her death. Bogart takes over the house
completely, beating Tara's father with a chain, and the future looks bleak for
all concerned.

**Review Summary:**
*Variety* (August 13, 1969) thought Jennifer "apparently uncertain as to what
her role is supposed to be."

*The New York Post* (February 4, 1971) merely said that Jennifer Jones had
returned to the screen after seven years "to an embarassment."

**Additional Sources:**
Reviews: *Film Daily*, August 18, 1969; *New York*, February 15, 1971; *New
York Daily News*, February 4, 1971; *The New York Times*, February 4,
1971; *The Villager*, August 21, 1969.
See Also: *Films and Filming*, July, 1973.

**Notes:**
What induced Jennifer Jones to accept the role of Astrid in this ludicrous film
is anybody's guess. It was an embarrassment for her once-loyal fans to hear

her casually remark to another player, "I made thirty stag films and never faked an orgasm." The film was virtually ignored when first released and didn't rate many reviews until re-released in 1971 as *Cult of the Damned*, when it played briefly in Manhattan as the lower half of a double bill.


F24    **THE TOWERING INFERNO**    (A 20th Century-Fox/Warner Bros. Production)

Released: December 10, 1974          Running Time: 165 minutes

**Cast:**
Steve McQueen (O'Hallorhan); Paul Newman (Doug Roberts); William Holden (Jim Duncan); Faye Dunnaway (Susan); Fred Astaire (Harlee Claiborne); Susan Blakely (Patty Simmons); Richard Chamberlain (Simmons); Jennifer Jones (Lisolette Mueller); O.J. Simpson (Security Chief Jernigan); Robert Vaughn (Senator Parker); Robert Wagner (Bigelow); Susan Flannery (Lorrie); Jack Collins (Mayor); Sheila Matthews (Mayor's wife); Normann Burton (Construction Chief); Carol McEvoy (Mrs. Albright); Michael Lookinland, Carlena Gower (Albright Children); John Crawford (Chief Engineer Callahan); Eric Nelson (Wes); Don Gordon (Fire Officer Kappy); Felton Perry (Scott); Ernie Orsatti (Mark); Olan Soule (Engineer).

**Credits:**
Director (John Guillermin); Producer (Irwin Allen); Screenplay (Stirling Silliphant, based on the novels of Richard Martin Stern and Thomas M. Scortia & Frank M. Robinson); Music (John Williams); Art Director (Ward Preston); Editors (Harold F. Kress, Carl Kress); Special Photographic Effects (L.B. Abbott); Stunt Coordinator (Paul Stander).

**Synopsis:**
San Francisco's newest building, the 138-story Glass Tower, is being dedicated, with hundreds of important people invited to attend the lavish dinner on the top floor. However, faulty wiring in the basement and the resulting short circuiting of wiring in an 81st floor storage room, causes the first flickers of a fire. The wiring problems in the basement reach the attention of Doug Roberts, the building's architect, who discovers that code requirements were not met properly by Roger Simmons, who was in charge of that phase of construction, although construction head James Duncan thought everything had been followed according to Roberts' plans. Meanwhile, as the fire begins to spread, Harlee Claiborne woos building resident Lisolette Mueller, inviting her to attend the swanky dedication dinner with him, his plan being to get her to invest in his phoney stock company. The fire, now burning out of control, is finally discovered and Roberts thinks everyone should be evacuated, but Duncan, not wanting to alarm the

important guests, decides not to. He thinks the fire department will handle the situation. When fire chief O'Halloran arrives and sees the seriousness of the fire, he overrides Duncan and demands that the guests be evacuated. The interior elevators are cut off by the fire, so the outside, scenic elevator is used, but it can hold only a few people at a time. Lisolette, worried about a deaf neighbor, reaches her floor by stairs, and rescues two children, but she has to make an arduous climb back up the broken stairs to the top floor. She and the children climb into the scenic elevator, but before it can safely reach the ground, an explosion shakes it loose from the cables and Lisolette plummets to her death. It appears that the remaining guests will also perish, but O'Halloran, in a last-ditch effort, lands on the building's roof and plants an explosive under a water tank. The tank explodes and the rushing water douses the fire, the suvivors are rescued and the building is saved.

**Review Summary:**
The *Hollywood Reporter* (December 16, 1974) complimented Jennifer for looking "fit and attractive" and for struggling "gamefully through tough physical ordeals."

*Variety* (December 18, 1974) termed Jennifer's performance "a fine return" and "extremely sympathetic."

**Additional Sources:**
Reviews: *BFI Monthly Film Bulletin*, February, 1975; *Christian Century*, March 5, 1975; *Commonweal*, April 11, 1975; *Films in Review*, February, 1975; *Independent Film Journal*, December 25, 1974; *Los Angeles Times*, December 15, 1974; *Motion Picture Herald Product Digest*, January 15, 1975; *New York*, January 13, 1975; *The New York Times*, February 4, 1975; *New Yorker*, December 30, 1974; *Newsweek*, December 30, 1974; *Time*, January 6, 1975.
See Also: *American Cinematographer*, February, 1975; *The Films of Steve McQueen*, *The Films of the 1970s*; *Magills Survey of Cinema*, Series II; *Reeling*.

**Notes:**
For her performance as Lisolette Mueller (a role first offered to Olivia de Havilland), Jennifer Jones was nominated for a Golden Globe as Best Supporting Actress of 1974. *The Towering Inferno* is Jennifer Jones's last film to date.

## 4
# Radio, Theatre, Television

Although it was apparently Jennifer Jones's greatest wish to become a stage actress, her film career far outweighs her career on the stage. Her major stage efforts are easily documented, but her early appearances in summer stock and her brief tenure with the Cherry Lane Theatre in New York City are more difficult to document. The same is true for her radio work in Oklahoma, although her guest appearances on various network programs during the 1940s are easily substantiated. Miss Jones has limited her television exposure to sporadic appearances on award presentations.


## RADIO

R1    *The Phylis Isley Radio Theatre* (October-December, 1938). KOME, Tulsa, Oklahoma.  A half-hour, weekly dramatic program that ran for 13 weeks.

R2    *Your Hollywood Newsgirl* (March 25, 1942). NBC. Jennifer Jones was introduced to radio listeners as the latest David O. Selznick discovery on this 15-minute news program.

R3    *The Pepsodent/Bob Hope Show* (January 11, 1944). NBC. She was presented a medal for her rise to stardom in *The Song of Bernadette.*

R4    *The Radio Hall of Fame* (February 20, 1944). NBC. Dramatization with Jennifer Jones, Charles Bickford, Helen O'Connell and Jerry Lester. Specific information not available.

R5    *United Nations Tribute to China* (July 8, 1944). NBC. A dramatization broadcast from Hollywood. Specific information not available.

R6    *Lux Radio Theatre* (October 16, 1944). NBC. Jennifer Jones and Van Johnson in a dramatization of *Seventh Heaven.*

R7   *The March of Dimes* (January 22, 1947).  NBC.  Appeared with other *Duel in the Sun* cast members of in a dramatization of the life of Philip Nolan and in appeal for the March of Dimes.

R8   *The Pepsodent/Bob Hope Show* (February 4, 1947).  NBC.  Reveived *Look* magazine's achievement award as Outstanding Actress of 1946.

R9   *Academy Awards* (March 21, 1956). NBC.  Sponsored by General Motors, Oldsmobile Division.  Jennifer Jones spoke briefly by recording.


**THEATRE**

R10   *The Phil Isley Stock Company, The Mansfield Players, The Harley Sadler Players* (1929-1937).  Numerous appearences with various summer stock companies.

R11   *The Cherry Lane Theatre* (October-November, 1938).  Greenwich Village, New York, New York.

Notes:
Jennifer Jones (then known as Phylis Isley) and Robert Walker had leading roles in several plays at this Off Off Broadway theatre, and were paid fifty cents each per performance.

R12   *Hello Out There* (September, 1941).  Lobrero Theatre, Santa Babara, California.

Notes:
In this one-act play (written by William Saroyan and directed by John Houseman), Jennifer Jones was cast as the female lead opposite Henry Bratsburg (Harry Morgan) at the insistence of Selznick, who wanted to gauge the audience reaction to his young discovery and assess her dramatic talent. He was pleased with the results.


R13   *Sarena Blandish*   (Summer, 1948).  La Jolla Playhouse, La Jolla, California.

Cast:
Information not available.


R14   *Portrait of a Lady* (December 21-25, 1954).  ANTA Theatre.  New York, New York.
Cast:

Jennifer Jones (Isabel Archer); Halliwell Hobbes (Mr. Touchett); Peter Pagan (Lord Warburton); Eric Fleming (Caspar Goodwood); Cathleen Nesbit (Countess Gemini); Robert Flemyng (Gilbert Osmond); Barbara O'Neil (Serena Merle); Douglas Watson (Ralph Touchett); Kathleen Comegys (Mrs. Touchett); Jan Farrand (Henrietta Stackpole); Marcia Morris (Pansy).

Review Summary:
*The New York Herald Tribune* (December 22, 1954), thought Jennifer Jones "technically immature" to properly portray the complex Isabel Archer.

*The New York Daily Mirror* (December 22, 1954) found her to be "gracious and graceful" as Isabel, and thought she achieved "genuine emotional impact" when the script permitted.

Notes:
The play closed on Christmas Day after four performances and its failure caused Selznick to cancel his plans to film the Henry James story. The play had first been seen in Boston's Colonial Theatre, where it opened on November 11, 1954, and played for a week and a half.


R15   *The Man With the Perfect Wife*   (March 22-27, 1965). Royal Poinciana Playhouse, Palm Beach, Florida.

Cast:
Information not available.

Review Summary:
Information not available.

Notes:
Following the run in Palm Beach, the play moved to Miami for another week's run, but Selznick deserted his plan to bring it to Broadway later in the year.


R16   *The Country Girl*   (September 29 - October 16, 1966) City Center, New York, New York.

Cast:
Rip Torn (Bernie Dodd); Joseph Anthony (Frank Elgin); Jennifer Jones (Georgie Elgin); Walter Allen (Larry); Jack Somack (Phil Cook); Richard Beymer (Paul Unger); Robin Strasser (Nancy Stoddard); Walter Lott (Ralph).
Review summary:

*The New York Times* (September 30, 1966) thought the performance of Jennifer Jones was "cool when it should be vital" and "petulant when it should be angry."

*Variety* (October 5, 1966) found Jennifer performance to be "artfully varied" and "touching," especially when considering her slight stage experience, limited rehearsal time and the lack of a try-out tour.

Notes:
*The Country Girl,* as part of the American Playwright Series, had a limited, two-week engagement. Franchot Tone was originally set to portray alcoholic actor Frank Elgin, but ill health forced him to withdraw from the production. Richard Beymer, who enacted the playwright's role, had appeared with Jennifer Jones in the 1954 film, *Indiscretion of an American Wife*, as her nephew, Paul.

## TELEVISION

R17    *The American Film Institute Tribute to Lillian Gish* (March 1, 1984). NBC. Jennifer Jones, who has worked with Miss Gish in two films, *Duel in the Sun*, 1946, and *Portrait of Jennie*, 1948, thanked the honoree for the pleasant memories of making those films.

R18    *The Academy of Motion Picture Arts and Sciences Awards Ceremony* (March 30, 1987). ABC. Jennifer Jones presented the Oscar for Best Cinematography to Chris Menges (*The Mission*).

R19    *The American Film Institute Tribute to Gregory Peck* (March 21, 1989). NBC. Peck's co-star in *Duel in the Sun*, 1946, and *The Man in the Gray Flannel Suit*, 1956, Jennifer Jones expressed her love for the actor and went on to say that performing love scenes with him had not been difficult.

# 5
# *Awards and Nominations*

## 1943

A1    **Academy Award** for Best Actress (*Song of Bernadette*).

A2    **Golden Globe** for outstanding performance (*Song of Bernadette*).

A3    **National Board of Review**'s best acting award for her performance as Bernadette Soubirous.

A4    **Outstanding Achievement Award** from *Look* magazine for *Song of Bernadette*.

## 1944

A5    **Academy Award** nomination for Best Supporting Actress (*Since You Went Away*).

## 1945

A6    **Academy Award** nomination for Best Actress (*Love Letters*).

## 1946

A7    **Academy Award** nomination for Best Actress (*Duel in the Sun*).

A8    **Oustanding Achievement Award** from *Look* magazine for *Duel in the Sun*.

## 1947

A9    **Sour Apple Award.** Voted least cooperative actress by the Hollywood Women's Press Club.

## 1949

A10  **Best Foreign Film Actress,** Paris Film Festival (*Madame Bovary*).

A11  **Film Francais Grand Prix des Directeurs de Cinema,** as voted by the theatre managers of France and North Africa (*Madame Bovary*).

## 1951

A12  **Patriotic Award** for her selfless act of visiting wounded American soldiers in Japan and Korea.

A13  **Citation** from The American Red Cross for compassion shown to wounded American soldiers.

A14  **Gold Medal** presented by General Van Fleet of the United Nations for boosting the morale of wounded American soldiers.

## 1955

A15  **Academy Award** nomination for Best Actress (*Love is a Many-Splendored Thing*).

A16  **Audie** as Most Popular Actress as voted by movie audiences.

A17  **Gold Medal Award** from *Photoplay* magazine as most popular actress.

## 1956

A18  **Motion Picture Award** from the California Federation of Women's Clubs for her performance in *Good Morning, Miss Dove*.

## 1974

A19  **Golden Globe** nomination as Best Supporting Actress (*The Towering Inferno*).

## 1985

A20  **Honored** by the University of Pennsylvania's School of Nursing for "promoting a fairer, more compassionate society."

## 6
# *Bibliography*

This bibliography does not purport to be a definitive listing of every print reference to actress Jennifer Jones. It does, however, offer an annotated list of books, magazine articles and a generous sampling of newspaper articles that deal with the life and/or career of Jones in some depth. Thumbnail biographical sketches are not included, nor are mentions in gossip and society columns. It is also virtually impossible for this bibliography to be current, as new film books (many including information on Jones) are being published literally every month.

## BOOKS

B001 Behlmer, Rudy, ed. *Memo From David O. Selznick.* New York: The Viking Press, 1972.

Extremely interesting look at the frequent -- and lengthy -- memos Selznick sent to directors and associates, many outlining specific directions as to how his wife, Jennifer Jones, should be costumed, photographed and directed.

B002 Bergen, Ronald, Graham Fuller and David Malcolm. *Academy Award Winners.* London: Multimedia Publications, Ltd., 1986.

This large format book, which provides an illustrated account of each year's ceremony and some analysis of the winning films and performances, devotes a couple paragraphs to Jennifer Jones and her 1943 Best Actress Oscar for *Song of Bernadette*, but uncovers nothing new, merely stating the facts.

B003 Bowers, Ronald. *The Selznick Players.* Cranbury, NJ: A.S. Barnes & Co., 1976.

An entertaining (and academic) look at the careers of the film stars managed by David O. Selznick, including Joan Fontaine, Ingrid Bergman and Jennifer Jones. The chapter on Jones covers her personal life and film career with detail and accuracy and offers some intelligent analysis as well.

B004  Brown, Peter H. *The Real Oscar; The Story Behind the Academy Awards*. Los Angeles: Rosebud Books, 1981.

Brown attempts to tell the "real" story behind the Academy Awards, why some films/performers win and others don't. According to Brown, the Jennifer Jones nominations were due, not to fine acting, but to Selznick's intense lobbying. Brown attributes her 1955 nomination for *Love is a Many-Splendored Thing* to an impressive, specially printed, golden ink ad in trade papers.

B005  Cameron, Ian and Elizabeth. *Dames*. New York: Praeger, 1969.

Includes a fairly brief, but informative chapter on Jennifer Jones, her life, her film career, and her importance as a film star.

B006  Chaneles, Sol and Albert Wolsky. *The Movie Makers*. Secaucus, NJ: Derbibooks, Inc., 1974.

A large book which includes a brief synopsis of Jones's career with a few movie highlights added.

B007  Clarke, Gerald. *Capote; A Biography*. New York: Ballantine Books, 1989.

An excellent biography of one of this century's best-known writers that contains several references to Jennifer Jones, especially in the chapters discussing Capote's foray into screenwriting. (He wrote dialogue for *Indiscretion of an American Wife* (1953) and *Beat the Devil* (1954), both starring Jones).

B008  Cotten, Joseph. *Joseph Cotten, an Autobiography; Vanity Will Get You Somewhere*. New York: Avon Books, 1987.

Joseph Cotten, who co-starred with Jennifer Jones in four films, mentions her often in his well-written memoirs, and always with respect and admiration. In one paragraph (page 138), which begins, "It seems to me that I have always known Jennifer Jones...," he succeeds in revealing more about this shy and reserved actress that most film historians have been able to do in several pages.

B009  Dowd, Nancy and David Shepard. *King Vidor*. Metuchen, NJ: Scarecrow Press and The Director's Guild of America, 1988.

In this published interview, director Vidor discusses his career as an American film director. Of his two films with Jones (*Duel in the Sun*, 1946, and *Ruby Gentry*, 1952), he had mixed memories: Selznick was a bad memory, but he complimented Jones on her ability to show inner feelings through facial expressions. Vidor recognized that quality as one that needed special handling and felt he knew best how it should be handled.

B010 Druxman, Michael. *Charlton Heston.* New York: Pyramid, 1976.

One of the Pyramid Illustrated History of the Movies series, this close examination of Heston's career includes some discussion of Jones's performance opposite Heston in *Ruby Gentry* (1952), which is described as being "stretched almost to the point of parody."

B011      Durgnat, Raymond and Scott Simmon. *King Vidor, American.* Berkeley, CA.: The University of California Press, 1988.

An academic look at director Vidor and his films which includes some discussion of Jones and her work for Vidor in *Duel in the Sun* (1946) and *Ruby Gentry* (1952), but offers little insight into her life apart from the characters she played in these films.

B012 Fontaine, Joan. *No Bed of Roses.* New York: William Morrow & Co., 1978.

Fontaine and Jones were both under contract to Selznick during the 1940s and she mentions Jones occasionally in this autobiography. She achieves some depth late in the book when she comments that Jones was perhaps the most insecure actress with whom she had ever worked. "Acting was torture to her," Fontaine says.

B013 Haver, Ronald. *David O. Selznick's Hollywood.* New York: Knopf, 1980.

An enormous tome, gorgeously and expensively produced, which offers a minutely detailed look at David O. Selznick and his films. His professional and personal relationship with Jennifer Jones is discussed at great length, as are the six Jones films which he personally produced. Sumptuously illustrated.

B014 Hirschhorn, Ken. *Rating the Movie Stars for Home Video, TV, Cable.* New York: Beekman House, 1983.

Sponsored by the editors of *Consumer Guide*, this book is impressive in the extraordinary number of motion picture performers included (411), but the system of rating the stars is rather disappointing and cannot be taken seriously. The author allegedly watched every film these 411 stars made, then rated their performances using a four star system, four stars being excellent, one star being poor, with varying fractions between. The scores were averaged for each star, and the results are often ludicrous -- Eddie Murphy gets four stars while Katharine Hepburn is given a three star rating. Jennifer Jones, with two-and-a-half stars, fares better than Ronald Reagan and Jerry Lewis, but falls *below* Betty Grable. As far as individual perfomances go, Hirschhorn liked Jones best (four stars) in *Cluny Brown* (1946), *Beat the Devil* (1954) and *The Barretts of Wimpole Street* (1957) and least (one star) in *Angel, Angel, Down We Go* (1969). A short biography is also included for each performer and of Jones, Hirschhorn writes, "a sensitive actress in good vehicles, but too often resorted to lip-twisting mannerisms."

B015  Hopper, Hedda and James Brough. *The Whole Truth and Nothing But*. New York: Doubleday, 1962.

An entertaining memoir by one of the gossip queens of old Hollywood. Miss Hopper has devoted an entire chapter to the sad tale of Robert Walker, and seems to blame his problems (without actually saying so) on his divorce from Jennifer Jones. She throws in a few pithy observations of Jones: shy, reticent, nervous when acting, and closes by saying it must be easy for Jennifer to remember "and mighty hard to forget."

B016  Huston, John. *An Open Book*. New York: Knopf, 1980.

The respected director includes some interesting and insightful commentary on Jennifer Jones in his autobiography. He found her a pleasure to direct and complimented her ability to put herself completely in the hands of the director. His opinion of Selznick's love for Jennifer was that it was "real and touching" but detrimental to his judgment. Selznick didn't do "anything worth a damn" after they were married, he says.

B017  Kaminsky, Stuart. *John Huston, Maker of Magic*. Boston: Houghton Mifflin Co., 1978.

Fairly routine mentions of Jones as a cast member in Huston's *We Were Strangers* (1949) and *Beat the Devil* (1954), but does include at least one intersting bit of trivia: Huston once had a pet terrier named Jenny in Jennifer's honor.

B018  Karney, Robyn. *The Movie Stars Story*. New York: Crescent Books, 1984.

Karney edited this impressively done encyclopedic volume in which other film historians and enthusiasts write about the movie stars. About Jennifer Jones, Joel Finler writes: "was discovered by producer David O.

Selznick and placed under contract in 1940." It was actually 1941, and although that error in Finler's too-brief summary of Jones's career is a minor one, nothing new, interesting or even exciting is brought to light.

B019 Katz, Ephraim. *The Film Enclycopedia*. New York: Putnam Publishing Group, 1979.

Quite possibly the best encyclopedic reference to motion pictures in print. In its 1,266 pages, one can find the career summaries of thousands of actors, directors, cameramen and others connected to the industry as well as thorough explanations of various film genres and techniques. The life/career of Jennifer Jones is -- not surprisingly -- allotted little space, but is surprisingly detailed. A complete filmography is included.

B020 Kobal, John. *Gods and Goddesses of the Movies*. New York: Crescent Books, 1973.

It was Selznick's goal to make Jennifer Jones a movie goddess, but she is not considered one by Kobal. He does, however, discuss two of her more romantic films -- *Portrait of Jennie* (1948) and *Madame Bovary* (1949). He characterizes Jones as a "screen fury," an actress who became popular playing a type contrary to her own personality.

B021 Leff, Leonard J. *Hitchcock and Selznick*. New York: Weidenfeld and Nicholson, 1987.

An academic look at the brief alliance of these two powerful and creative men, from which came such cinema classics as *Spellbound* (1945) and *Notorious* (1946). Jennifer Jones, as Selznick's protegee and wife, figures prominently in this study, but she is treated only as the object of Selznick's obsession and appears rather one-dimensional.

B022 Levy, Emanuel. *And the Winner is...* New York: Ungar Publishing Co., 1987.

Jennifer Jones (an Oscar winner of 1943) is mentioned briefly in this expose of the political nature of the Oscars, but the references to her are not particularly flattering. Her Academy Award for *Song of Bernadette* was due, says Levy, not to talent so much as to having found the "right role and director." He also considers her 1946 nomination for *Duel in the Sun* unworthy, attributing it to Selznick's influence.

B023 Linet, Beverly. *Star-Crossed; The Story of Robert Walker and Jennifer Jones*. New York: G.P. Putnam's Sons, 1986.

A fascinating, highly entertaining and enlightening book, thoroughly chronicling the life and career of Walker and Jones. Linet closely examines their childhood, marriage (which is pictured as idyllic), their simultaneous rise to movie stardom and subsequent break-up. Linet treats Walker more sympathetically than Jones, who left him for David O. Selznick. Robert Walker was left broken hearted and disillusioned and suffered several emotional breakdowns before his premature death in 1951. It is Linet's conclusion that Jones was more attracted by the power of Selznick than to the selfless love offered by Walker. Jones is unquestionably the villain in this well-researched biography which is rather depressing in its depiction of Walker and his sad, tormented life.

B024    Lloyd, Ann and Graham Fuller. *The Illustrated Who's Who of the Cinema*. New York: Portland House, 1987.

Includes a brief summary of Jennifer Jones's career with a few movie highlights.

B025    McDowall, Roddy, ed. *Double Exposure*. New York: Delacorte Press, 1966.

McDowall edited this fine book in which celebrities write about other celebrities. Henry Miller has written a touching tribute to Jennifer Jones, a true fan letter in which he admits that had seen her in nothing more than *Good Morning, Miss Dove*, he would never have forgotten her.

B026    MacPherson, Don and Louise Brody. *Leading Ladies*. New York: Crescent Books, 1986.

A glossy, impressive collection of short essays and glamour shots of seven decades worth of leading ladies of the silver screen. In the well-written and slightly analytical essay on Jennifer Jones, she is compared to Norma Shearer as a "species of Hollywood royalty to whom critical standards are hardly applicable." The only error is the reference to her contract with Selznick having been signed in 1940. It was actually 1941, but that's a picayune flaw in an otherwise splendid piece.

B027    Madsen, Axel. *William Wyler*. New York: Thomas Y. Crowell Co., 1973.

Wyler directed Jennifer Jones in *Carrie* (1952), and in this biography, he relates a few details from the experience, primarily that Jones was pregnant at the time but insisted on binding herself in tight corsets. He mentions her unfortunate miscarriage following the film's completion, but won't go as far as to say the corsets were the cause.

B028  Masters, George and Norma Lee Browning. *The Masters Way to Beauty*. New York: E.P. Dutton & Co., 1977.

Masters, a well-known beauty consultant for several Hollywood stars, makes the startling statement in his memoirs that Jennifer Jones looks better undressed and Cyd Charisse looks better fully clothed. It's hard to beat that remark, but he does describe -- in fascinating detail -- the beauty rituals of Miss Jones. Much of what he says seems a bit exaggerated (a room larger than most living rooms just for her cosmetics; spending thousands of dollars a year on facial creams, using each variety only once before throwing it out...), but he says he was there.

B029  Mordden, Ethan. *The Hollywood Studios*. New York: Alfred A. Knopf, Inc., 1988.

An analysis of the Hollywood studios, from the supreme MGM to the independent Selznick International. David O. Selznick's attempt to make a cinema immortal of Jennifer Jones is rather incorrectly compared to Samuel Goldwyn and Anna Sten, Arthur Freed and Lucille Bremer, and L.B. Mayer and Ginny Simms. Sten, Bremer and Simms may have fallen short of their mentors' expectations, but one can hardly call Jennifer Jones a failure. Mordden is particularly critical of Jones, whom he says had no charisma as an actress.

B030  Moshier, Franklyn. *The Films of Jennifer Jones*. San Francisco: W. Franklyn Moshier, 1978.

Very similar in format to the Citadel "Films of..." series, this lavishly illustrated book offers a complete look at Jennifer Jones -- a surprisingly detailed biography, and interesting production information on her 23 films and one serial, including complete cast and credits, author's notes and contemporary reviews. A wonderful source for information, but a listing of her theatre work would have been helpful.

B031  Osborne, Robert. *Academy Awards Illustrated*. Hollywood: Marvin Miller Enterprises, 1965.

One of the first books to delve into Oscar's past and expose the backstage jealousy, excitement and disappointment. Osborne admirably assesses each year's ceremony (up to 1964), writing about the contenders and winners in an entertaining and highly readable style. A full-page bio is included for each winning performer (supporting Oscar winners rate only a picture, however), and about Jones, 1943's Best Actress, he writes that she "is a Hollywood mystery" and has become "less known as a public personality each year." Illustrations include a lovely still from *Song of Bernadette* and a candid of the year's winners.

B032  Parish, James Robert. *The Glamour Girls*. New Rochelle, NY:
        Arlington House, 1975.

An excellent book (up to Parish's usual standards) in which the careers
of Joan Bennett, Rita Hayworth, Audrey Hepburn, Kim Novak and Jennifer
Jones are covered in minute detail.  About Jones, Parish writes that her
career is "badly in need of re-evaluation." He makes the interesting statement
that her screen persona is "an acquired taste, requiring patience, open-
mindedness and a willingness to explore the visually and emotionally
offbeat."  The chapter brings Jones up to 1974 and her role as the widow in
*The Towering Inferno*.

B033  Paul, William. *Ernst Lubitsch's American Comedy*. New York:
        Columbia University Press, 1983.

The *Village Voice* hailed this book as a "momumental work," and
indeed the American career of director Ernst Lubitsch is analyzed with great
skill.  *Cluny Brown*, starring Jennifer Jones, was his last completed film, and
the film -- and Jennifer's role -- are discussed at great length.   Paul
characterizes Jones as an actress who is sexual "without being aware of her
own sexuality."

B034  Peary, Danny, ed. *Close-Ups*. New York:  Workman Publishing
        Co., 1978.

Very similar to McDowall's *Double Exposure*. Peary has edited a
compilation of essays written about film stars by their friends, co-workers
and, in some cases, family members. In a chapter titled "Jennifer Jones:
Tempting Fate," Bill Horrigan closely examines her career, paying
particular attention to the heroines she portrayed, from the genteel
Bernadette, Miss Dove and Elizabeth Barrett Browning, to the sensual and
florid Pearl Chavez, Emma Bovary and Ruby Gentry.  He characterizes the
"Jones women" as women who act upon their desires, explaining why they
are so often oppressed, penalized and headed for a bad end.  Horrigan's
favorite Jones performance seems to be Emma Bovary, which, he says
"makes everything she did before seem like a rehearsal."  The Selznick
influence is discussed but Horrigan makes it clear that to examine Jones *only*
as Selznick's protegee is a misconception "of the most disreputable kind."

B035  Quirk, Lawrence J. *Claudette Colbert, an Illustrated Biography*.
        New York:  Crown, 1985.

Quirk, one of the more prolific of star biographers, does an excellent
job of chronicling the life of Claudette Colbert, a much-respected actress
who portrayed the mother of Jennifer Jones in the 1944 *Since You Went
Away*. Quirk quotes John Cromwell, the film's director, as saying that
Jennifer was upset during most of the filming due to Selznick's personal

interest in her, her marriage troubles, her role, and "just about everything." He says with all her worries it is amazing that Jennifer got through the film at all, and is particularly complimentary of her performance.

B036  Quirk, Lawrence J. *The Great Romantic Films.* Secaucus, NJ:
      Citadel Press, 1974.

An insightful, entertaining discussion of fifty romantic American films, from *Smilin' Through* (1932) to *Love and Pain and the Whole Damn Thing* (1973). Included are the Jennifer Jones films *Portrait of Jennie* (1948) and *The Barretts of Wimpole Street* (1957), and Quirk offers some interesting analysis of Jones's performances in each film. He admits to being fonder of Jones than most film historians and considers her performances often remarkable, indicative of "considerable depth, range and virtuosity."

B037  Ragan, David. *Movie Stars of the 40s.* Englewood Cliffs, NJ:
      Prentice Hall, 1985.

Ragan has chosen a good cross-section of popular film stars from the 1940s and has admirably (although briefly) summarized their careers, throwing in some interesting trivia and movie highlights. He gets the facts right in his Jennifer Jones entry, and makes the interesting observation that Selznick thought she was the "equivalent of the Hope diamond, perfection in every facet..."

B038  Selznick, Irene Mayer. *A Private View.* New York: Alfred A.
      Knopf, Inc., 1983.

The daughter of L.B. Mayer and the first wife of David O. Selznick, Irene Mayer Selznick did indeed have a private view of Hollywood during its formative years, and in this well-written and informative autobiography, there are surprisingly few mentions of Jennifer Jones, with whom Selznick became obsessed, bringing his first marriage to an end. The first Mrs. Selznick seems to feel no animosity toward the second Mrs. Selznick, and even admits that there was already something "deeply wrong with the marriage," that if it hadn't been Jennifer, "it would have been someone else."

B039  Shipman, David. *The Great Movie Stars; the International Years.*
      Hill and Wang, 1972.

A companion edition to Shipman's *The Great Movie Stars; the Golden Years*, this book offers detailed biographical and career information of film stars from the Second World War to the 1970s. In his lengthy chapter on Jennifer Jones, Shipman states that following her rise to stardom as Bernadette, she went on to appear in several other films "with only medium success." He makes the puzzling remark that although her chief virtue was not being the standard Hollywood female, her failing was that she "wasn't quite anything else, either."

B040  Swann, Thomas Burnett. *The Heroine or the Horse.* South
Brunswick, NJ: A.S. Barnes, 1977.

Swann has chronicled the careers of the heroines of Republic westerns, devoting a great deal of space to those actresses who achieved fame after leaving the Republic sagebrush behind. Jennifer Jones (as Phylis Isley) had appeared in the 1939 Republic western, *New Frontier*, and Swann accurately details her life and mentions many of her later film roles. Her relationship with Selznick also rates several inches of copy.

B041  Thomas, Bob . *Golden Boy; the Untold Story of William Holden.*
New York: St. Martin's Press, 1983.

An interesting biography in which Thomas discusses Holden's working relationship with Jennifer Jones during the filming of *Love is a Many-Splendored Thing* (1955). It was apparently not a happy one.

B042  Thomas, Bob. *Selznick.* New York: Doubleday, 1971.

A magnificent biography of David O. Selznick which thoroughly discusses his relationship -- personal and professional -- with Jennifer Jones. Thomas does include one incident which does not appear in other sources, and which cannot be substantiated -- that Phylis Isley (before being re-christened Jennifer Jones) replaced Dorothy McGuire one night during the Broadway run of *Claudia*. According to Thomas, the cast members were hostile toward her, but her performance impressed Selznick to the point of offering her a contract.

B043  Thomas, Tony. *The Films of the Forties.* Secaucus, NJ: Citadel
Press, 1975.

In the usual Citadel style, 100 films from the 1940s are thoroughly discussed and analyzed. Two films starring Jennifer Jones (*Duel in the Sun*, 1946, and *Portrait of Jennie*, 1948) are included and Thomas briefly discusses her performances in each.

B044  Thomson, David. *A Biographical Dictionary of the Cinema.*
London: Martin, Secker and Warburg, Ltd., 1975.

Offers a brief, but accurate and interesting account of Jennifer Jones, her life and career, and even includes some insightful analysis: her work is described a erratic, just as her nature "seems torn between decorous and sensual impulses"; as Pearl Chavez, the primitive power of the film is said to emanate from her "like blood from a wound." Thomson calls Pearl Chavez "the Hyde of a generally Jeckyll-natured actress."

B045  Wlaschin, Ken. *The Illustrated Enclyclopedia of the World's Great Movie Stars.* New York: Harmony Books, 1979.

A slickly done book which selects 400 of the most important film stars from all times and countries and discusses the reasons why they became stars, evaluates their importance today, and lists their ten best films (according to the reviews and opinions of film critics.) The career of Jennifer Jones is discussed briefly but impressively. It is interesting to note that *Since You Went Away* (1944), for which Jones received an academy award nomination, is *not* listed among her ten best films, while *Carrie* (1952), for which she received mixed reviews, is.


## MAGAZINE ARTICLES

B046  "Academy Awards." *Movie Stars Parade.* May, 1944, p. 32-33.

A report in words and pictures of the Academy Awards ceremony on March 2, 1944. Two shots of Jennifer are included, and she is quoted as saying that winning the Oscar was the "most wonderful birthday present I've ever received."

B047  Arnold, Maxine. "The Amazing Miss Jones." *Photoplay.* January, 1946,  pp 36, 86-87.

A charming profile of Jennifer Jones that presents her as a dedicated actress, a loving mother and a sweet-natured girl from Oklahoma. What's most "amazing" about the actress profiled here is that she is said to eat five meals a day without gaining weight! Her love-life is not mentioned.


B048  Arnold, Maxine. "Jennifer -- The Fabulous Life of a Girl Named Jones." *Photoplay.* September, 1947,  pp 64-67, 118-121.

A "fabulous" article that richly details the childhood of Jennifer Jones, then brings her up to 1947, to the filming of *Portrait of Jennie.* An obviously well-researched article that is well-written and entertaining.


B049  Baskette, Kirtley. "Bob Walker's Life Story, Part One." *Modern Screen.* January, 1946, pp 32-35, 88-94.

An amazingly detailed and fascinating account of Walker's early childhood and his one year at the American Academy of Dramatic Arts in

New York. His romance with fellow student Phylis Isley is fully developed and accurately presented.

B050   Baskette, Kirtley. "Bob Walker's Life Story, Part Two." *Modern Screen*. February, 1946,  pp 38-39, 97, 100-109.

Concludes with Walker winning the part of playing Jerome Kern in MGM's *Till the Clouds Roll By*, but begins with his aborted second year at AADA and his touching proposal to Phylis Isley in Central Park.  Their struggle to find stage work, their trials and joys, and their marriage in Tulsa are skillfully handled. The story becomes questionable at this point and their life in Hollywood is not written about with the same rich flavor for detail. Jennifer disappears from the story after their separation, the reasons for which, Baskette explains, are not known.

B051   Beatty, Jerome. "Keeping Up with the Jones Girl." *American Magazine*.  October, 1944,  pp 28-29, 108-110.

A fascinating look at Jennifer Jones, her early life, her experiences in New York, and her marriage to Robert Walker, whose life is also chronicled, although in less detail. The "perfect marriage" publicity angle for *Song of Bernadette*, and the backfire of that publicity, presents an intertesting picture of how the studios created certain images for their stars.

B052   Bentley, Janet. "Jennifer Jones -- Please Read." *Photoplay*. March, 1944,  pp 38, 92-94.

An open letter to Jennifer Jones, criticizing her for breaking up with Robert Walker. Bentley relates several details from their romance, building it up to be idyllic, then charges the actress with "wounding more people than you can possibly guess" by deciding to separate from Walker. Bentley urges Jones to "please read this, and then think, just a little longer." This article can serve as an example of how the Jones/Walker separation and divorce affected their fans.

B053   "Bright Boy." *Modern Screen*.  December, 1944,  pp 61-63.

Another rendition of the Walker/Jones romance, marriage and separation.  However, this one ends on an optimistic note by saying the marriage may be mended bcause it was "built on rock, not sand."

B054   Carey, Rebecca. "Jennifer Jones Speaks for Herself." *Photoplay*. September, 1945,  pp 29, 116-117.

A rather brief, but interesting article which begins by recounting testimony from the Walker/Jones divorce hearing, then launches into an interview with Jennifer who never once mentions Walker or the divorce but talks a great deal about motherhood, her personality, Hollywood and her film roles.

B055 Carpozi, George. "I Tried to Die." *Photoplay*. February, 1968,
    pp. 10-11, 98.

Carpozi tries to analyze Jones's suicide attempt on November 9, 1967, but merely lists every sorrow Jones has had to face (growing older, being widowed, the break-up of her first marriage, the recent dearth of film offers, suffering a miscarriage, etc), and doesn't arrive at a conclusion.

B056 "Cluny Brown." *Silver Screen*. July, 1946,  p. 46.

A page-full of pictures from the film with accompanying article that touts Jennifer's comedic abilities, heretofore hidden in "somber, dramatic parts."

B057 Colby, Anita. "That Dream Girl Jones." *Photoplay*.  September, 1946, pp 46,74,76.

A somewhat corny tribute to Jones that drips with compliments. According to Colby, Jones is the best-hearted, most agreeable and best-humored actress in Hollywood.  The article was probably intended to counteract the rather unfavorable publicity Jones was receiving due to her sensual role in Selznick's *Duel in the Sun*.

B058 Crichton, Kyle. "The Name is Jones." *Colliers*.  April 24, 1943,
    pp  78, 81.

A rather superficial but nonetheless interesting profile of the "newcomer" who had won the most coveted role of 1943, that of Saint Bernadette.  Crichton repeats the oft-told tale of her "discovery" in Selznick's office, but openly admits that he doesn't believe it.  He does apparantly believe the Selznick publicity that *The Song of Bernadette* would be Jones's first time before a movie camera.

B059 *Current Biography*. 1944, pp 328-331.

A long, detailed and extremely impressive biography (the most extensive of Jennifer Jones up to that time) that illustrates how important a personality she was considered. As Jennifer Jones, she had only appeared in two films at this time, but much was expected of her. The unnamed biographer obviosuly did a great deal of research, and the only error was having she and Walker re-enroll for a second term at AADA, which they did not do.

B060  Doyle, Neil.  "Jennifer Jones."  *Films in Review*.  August/September, 1961,  pp 390-400.

A solid Jones biography and career summary that covers familiar ground, but does so in a professional manner.  Doyle includes some analysis and terms Jones's career "one of the oddest in motion picture history," then explains why.

B061  Dudley, Fredda.  "Sunday Pop."  *Movie Stars Parade*.  April, 1945, pp  54-55, 79-81.

A sympathetic profile of Robert Walker built around his visitation rights which were limited to Sunday afternoons.  Asked why he did not seek joint custody of his two sons, he explained that kids "belong with their mother."  And he discusses their mother openly, without malice, terming her one of the finest dramatic actresses in the business.  He does say that he has been a little disturbed over her "goody, goody roles"  and thinks a change of pace might do her good, "playing Amber in *Forever Amber*."  The rumor that the marriage might be mended isn't discussed, but he does say it would be nice to live at home again, "instead of being a Sunday pop."

B062  "Duel in the Sun."  *Movie Stars Parade*.  April, 1946, pp  56-57.

A double-page spread of candid production shots of Selznick's western epic.  Includes several pictures of Jennifer Jones in --and out -- of costume.

B063  "The 59th Academy Awards."  *Films in Review*.  May, 1987,  pp 292-293.

A brief summary of the awards ceremony which includes a description of Jennifer Jones (one of the presenters) as "nervous" and "barely recognizeable."

B064  "Film-Radio Feud over Guest Stars Highlight's Tomorrow's Television."  *Newsweek*.  April 3, 1944,  pp 82,84.

A report on the growing rift between movies and radio concerning the guest appearances of cinema stars and the question, which medium gains and which loses?  The question is posed, will television cause a similar problem?  Jennifer Jones is mentioned as being a victim of the feud, her scheduled appearance on CBS' *Star and the Story* being first re-scheduled, then cancelled.

B065  Graham, Sheila.  "Robert Walker; Tragic Figure."  *Modern Screen*.  January, 1949,  pp  39, 84-85.

A sympathetic profile of Walker in which Graham discusses his failed marriage to Jennifer Jones and his ensuing emotion problems. Jennifer is not blamed for his unhappiness, but his torch-carrying is. Walker is himself interviewed, and although he won't comment on the reasons behind the separation and divorce, he does say that the first wedge in the marriage was hammered in by the press who insisted Jennifer was single when she was first cast as Bernadette.

B066  Hall, Gladys. "Who is Jennifer Jones?" *Silver Screen*.  August, 1943,  pp  30, 61-62,  64.

Touted as the first confidential interview with the young unknown who was currently filming *Song of Bernadette*, this article is crammed with quotes from Jennifer Jones about her likes and dislikes.  Hall fills in Jennifer's background with rich detail, but leaves out her previous filmwork at Republic.  When Jennifer is asked about her *Claudia* audition, she said she hadn't thought about motion pictures, "didn't suppose I had enough experience for them."

B067  "Heading Up." *Movie Stars Parade*.  April, 1943, p. 45.

A full-page photo of Jennifer Jones and an accompanying biographical paragraph designed to introduce her to the readers as an actress "heading up" stardom's ladder.  She had just begun filming *Bernadette*, and overnight stardom is predicted for the actress who is likened to Teresa Wright, "only taller."  A brief synopsis of her thespic experience is included (no mention of her work for Republic) and although her marriage is casually mentioned, her husband's name isn't.

B068  "Heading Up." *Movie Stars Parade*.  July, 1943, p. 38.

A photo and brief biography of Robert Walker, MGM's newest golden-haired boy, who was "heading up" to stardom. In the three months since Jennifer Jones appeared in this monthly feature, the ban on mentioning their marriage was apparently lifted because Walker's marriage to Jennifer plays an important part in this article.

B069  "Heading Up." *Movie Stars Parade*.  February, 1944, p. 39.

Jennifer Jones and Robert Walker were pictured together in this feature, but they were already living apart.  The accompanying article explains their separation by saying that although they could struggle through hardships together, they can't "buck what sometimes hardest -- good fortune."

B070  "Here's to the Ladies." *Screen Greats*.  Summer, 1971, p. 32.

A one-page synopsis of Jennifer Jones, her life and career, that mentions several high and low points, but never manages to rise above the ordinary.

B071 Hume, Rod. "She Saw the Vision -- and Became a Star." *Films and Filming*. June, 1956, p. 15.

The "vision" is what she saw when a stick was waved behind a movie camera during her screen test for *Song of Bernadette*. This article not only recounts that story but offers an interesting profile of the actress and her career (but, oddly enough, doesn't mention her work for Republic). According to Hume, Jones has made fewer films than any other top ranking star in a comparable period, but, he adds, she has "never made a film which lacked distinction."

B072 "Jennifer Goes West." *Movie Stars Parade*. November, 1945, p. 44.

A beautifully tinted, full page photo of Jennifer Jones as Pearl Chavez. The lengthy caption predicts that her role in film, *Duel in the Sun*, the first role to remove her from "movie goodness," will earn her a second Oscar. Erroneously states that, as Phylis Isley, she was once the "cactus epic queen."

B073 "Jennifer Jones." *Films and Filming*. November, 1987, p. 10.

One of those question-and-answer columns in which a reader inquires as to Jennifer's whereabouts since *The Towering Inferno*. The answer is a brief summary of what Miss Jones has been doing since her last film appearance in 1974, i.e., buying treasures for her husband's art museum.

B074 "Jennifer Jones." *Life*. December 13, 1948.

Beneath a full-page photo, in which Jennifer models a new Christian Dior gown, appears a brief profile, listing some of the titles she has been voted: The Enamel Girl; 1947's Most Uncooperative Actress, etc.

B075 "Jennifer Jones." *Modern Screen*. November, 1944, p. 20.

A brief profile of the actress (accompanied by a lovely color portrait) that offers two versions of how she got the name "Jennifer Jones," airs rumor that she has been dating Fox producer Watson Webb, and reveals her intentions of someday acting with Spencer Tracy and Charles Boyer. It is the author's opinion that Jones should have had more experience before achieving sudden fame, that she has not adjusted well to its pressures. The article ends with the puzzling statement that she has proven actresses are"born not made" through such films as *Since You Went Away* and *Keys to the Kingdom.* (While it is true that at the time Selznick signed her she was considered for *Keys*, the film was eventually made without her).

B076 Kinkead, Jean. "Kid Brother." *Modern Screen.* September, 1946, pp 54-55, 111,114.

The article's main concern is Robert Walker's relationship with his older brothers, but his romance and marriage to Jennifer Jones is also mentioned.

B077 "Lavish, Lusty Western." *Silver Screen.* May, 1946, p. 46.

A two-page spread of location photos from *Duel in the Sun.* Several shots of Jennifer Jones with captions explaining her role.

B078 Leslie, Leon. "The New Jennifer Jones." *Screen Stars.* January, 1945, pp 12-13, 58-59.

Begins as a flowery description of Jennifer Jones and her rise to stardom and then becomes interesting as Jennifer talks about herself, her first two film roles, her confidence in David O. Selznick, her fear of live radio and her two sons.

B079 Lewis, Emory. "Portrait of Jennifer." *Cue.* December 4, 1954, p. 16.

Lewis discusses Jones's upcoming Broadway debut in *Portrait of Lady*, of which much was expected. Jennifer is quoted as saying she would "burst into tears" if people didn't like her in the role. Sadly, she wasn't liked and the play closed after seven performances.

B080 "Life Goes on Location with a Western." *Life.* April 23, 1945, pp 97-99.

A look at the location filming of *Duel in the Sun*, and also a look at the location site, 41 miles from Tuscon, Arizona. Several candid shots of Jennifer Jones with captions explaining her actions.

B081 "Life's Cover." *Life.* July 24, 1944, p. 11.

A portrait of Jennifer Jones graces the cover of this issue, and the small, inside article praises the actress for her "warm and sensitive performances" in *Song of Bernadette* and *Since You Went Away.*

B082 "Look Presents Achievement Award." *Look.* February 18, 1947.

Jones was awarded a motion picture achievement award because she was considered "one of the most talented" young dramatic actresses, and because of her "vivid acting" in *Duel in the Sun*. The brief article also includes flattering quotes from King Vidor and William Dieterle.

B083  Lowrance, Dee. "Portrait of Jenny." *Modern Screen*.  March, 1948, pp  30-31, 79, 81-82.

An interview with Jennifer Jones in which she talks about her newest film, *Portrait of Jennie*, currently in production.  She is described by Lowrance as an "enigma with a special, wraithlike quality of separateness." Lowrance also writes about the star's shyness, but only of publicity, and insists that Jennifer truly likes people and is always willing to help people in need.  As an example, she tells how, during the War, a tired Jennifer had spent 18 hours helping with a Nurse's Aid seminar in Indianapolis yet still visited with a train-load of wounded soldiers, laughing and singing with them, for an additional three hours!

B084  Mann, May. "Going Hollywood." *Screen Stars*.  December, 1946, pp  28-29, 48.

A gossip column, a regular feature in the magazine, which tells where the stars have been seen, and who they were seen with...  On this occasion, Jennifer Jones was observed lunching at Santa Monica's Cobana Club with Daryl Zanuck.  A photo is offered as proof.

B085  Mason, Jerry. "Jennifer Jones and Bob Walker are the Original Mr. and Mrs. Cinderella." *This Week*.  November 21, 1943, pp 28-29.

An innocuous interview with Jennifer and Robert, interesting because they tell their own story, though very quickly; however, some of what they are quoted as saying contradicts what was later known to be fact, i.e., Jennifer says she "ran almost all the way" to see Mr. Selznick when called back for an interview.  It's pleasant reading nonetheless, and all seems well and happy at the Walker home.

B086  Maxwell, Ella. "Hollywood Show-offs." *Photoplay*.  December, 1949,  pp  35, 104.

Miss Maxwell discusses several stars whom she considers "show-offs," among them Joan Fontaine, Robert Mitchum and Joan Crawford, then contrasts them with Jennifer Jones who is "shy to a fault." She describes Jones as an actress who is so uncomfortable during interviews that she "sits and pulls one hair after another out of her head."

B087  Maxwell, Ella. "Jennifer Jones: My Paradoxical Friend." *Photoplay*.

April, 1946, pp 34, 74.

Miss Maxwell discusses a party Selznick gave in Jennifer's honor, and relates how she watched the young actress interacting with the guests. She compliments Jennifer on her maturity as a woman, being no longer the innocent, naive girl for whom acting was the most important thing in life. The divorce from Robert Walker is mentioned, but Miss Maxwell is already predicting that Jones and Selznick will marry.

B088  Maxwell, Ella. "New Horizons." *Photoplay.* November, 1949.

With Jennifer Jones and David Selznick married, it was "safe" for the columnist to discuss their long romance, and Miss Maxwell does just that, admitting that she had known for years of their love, and had sensed the "mesmeric attraction between them" long before they made it public  She gives a few details of their wedding, touches on Jennifer's shyness, and ends with their being introduced to the Duke and Duchess of Windsor.

B089  "Meet Two Rising Stars." *Ladies Home Journal.* January, 1944,
      pp 85-87, 98.

This was where readers first learned that the Walker/Jones marriage was in trouble. Their separation is handled with sensitivity, and even with optimism.

B090  "Milestones." *Time.* June 14, 1971, p 77.

A brief news announcement of Jennifer's marriage to Norton Simon.

B091  "Miracle Girl." *American Magazine.* May, 1943, pp 28-29.

A brief biography of Jennifer Jones -- illustrated with several color shots of her gardening, listening to a Schubert recording, mending a blouse, making orage juice at breakfast, etc. -- that barely scratches the surface. The uncredited author presents Jennifer as a promising young actress with drive and ambition, but does make it appear, however, that testing for *Bernadette* was *her* idea.

B092  "Mr. and Mrs. Cinderella." *Movie Stars Parade.* November, 1943,
      pp 39-40, 70.

A pleasant (and accurate) story of two young people who meet at AADA, attend classes together, discuss acting technique together, and declare their love for each other on the Staten Island Ferry. They story brings them to California, where Jennifer is filming *Song of Bernadette* and where Bob has landed a good role in *Bataan*.

B093  "Movie of the Week: *Since You Went Away.*" *Life.* July 24, 1944,
      pp 53-55.

      Brief article on the film, explaining the story behind the motion
picture and a few details as to how it came to be filmed. Accompanied by a
two-page spread of stills, many of Jennifer Jones, who is singled out and
praised for her moving performance as the elder daughter.

B094  "Movies: Bernadette Works Another Miracle as Unknown
      Clicks
      in Werfel Role." *Newsweek.* February 7, 1944, pp 75-76.

      Tells Bernadette's story and how Franz Werfel happened to write it,
then praises Jennifer's "luminous spirituality and simplicity" in her
portrayal. A few details of Jennifer's private life are here too, including her
troubled marriage to Robert Walker.

B095  Muir, Florabel. "6 to 5 on Jones." *Modern Screen.* April, 1947,
      pp 38-39, 88, 90.

      After predicting that Jennifer Jones will win the Oscar for her
performance in *Duel in the Sun*, the article lapses into the usual interview,
including a full description of what Jones was wearing, how her house is
furnished, and what she like to eat. Miss Muir does manage to sneak in a few
insightful observations now and then, i.e., likening Selznick and Jones to
Pygmalion and Galatea, remarking on Selznick's tendency to "take
possession" of his stars, etc. Miss Jones also has a few interesting things to
say, such as calling her method of acting a form of "self hypnosis."

B096  Muir, Florabel. "The Mystery of Bob Walker." *Modern Screen.*
      June, 1948, pp 38-39, 105.

      A not-too-close look at Robert Walker's erratic behavior, his life in
Hollywood, his career (which he seems to have abandoned) and his social life.
Miss Muir states that "until not too long ago" Walker had hoped that he and
Jennifer might reconcile their differences.

B097  "Odd Twos." *Movie Stars Parade.* August, 1944, p. 63.

      A regular gossip column which pictured stars out together who were
not known to be a couple. Jennifer Jones and ex-publicist Lt. Bob Taplinger
were seen together at the Mocambo.

B098  "Newsmakers." *Newsweek.* June 14, 1971, p. 56.

      A brief, humorous description of the whirlwind romance and early
morning marriage of Norton Simon and Jennifer Jones.

B099  Parsons, Louella O.  "Bob Walker Talks About Jennifer Jones."
      *Photoplay*. November, 1944, pp 30-31, 83-84.

Walker talks to Miss Parsons about Jennifer, their marriage, and their
eminent divorce, but not once does he mention Selznick and he confesses that
he doesn't know what caused the break-up.  He does say that "we never had
any trouble or any words" until they moved to Hollywood.  Parsons ends by
merely asking the reader "what do you think?" as to whether or not Bob
Walker wants Jennifer back as his wife.

B100  Parsons, Louella O.  "I Predict a Honeymoon."  *Photoplay*. February,
      1949, pp 32-33, 74.

Miss Parsons predicts that David Selznick and Jennifer Jones will be
man and wife before the end of the year, and that the marriage will be
performed in either London or Paris.  The article segues into an interview
with Miss Jones during which the actress talks openly -- but not too candidly -
- about her relationship with Selznick, her relunctance to give interviews,
and about her two sons.  Interestingly enough, Jennifer never says that she
*loves* Selznick, it is Miss Parsons who says (many times) that Jennifer is a
"woman in love," that she thinks David "is a God," and that "she would rather
be miserable with David, than happy with any other man."

B101  "Passing Parade."  *Movie Stars Parade*. March, 1944, p. 8.

A full-page of pictures showing celebrities arriving at LA's Carthay
Circle for the premier of *Song of Bernadette* .  Jennifer was reported to be
too ill to attend.

B102  "Passing Parade."  *Movie Stars Parade*. October, 1944,  pp 44-45.

The stars turn out for the premier of *Since You Went Away* and are
captured for this double-page spread of candid photos.  Jennifer Jones was
there, and is well represented in the photo lay-out.  The most striking is a shot
of dark-haired Jennifer chatting with a very blonde Lana Turner at the post-
premier party at Trocadero.

B103  Peck, Gregory.  "Jenny and Miss Jones."  *Photoplay*. June, 1944,
      pp  44-45, 76.

A nice tribute to Jones from Peck, her co-star in *Duel in the Sun*.  He
describes her as a girl with tremendous courage and as an actress not afraid
of hard work.  She has a dual personality, he says: artist and girl.  Peck
includes some interesting commentary on her work at the La Jolla Playhouse
and her sense for practical jokes, a side of her personality usually well-
hidden.

B104  Pieck, Kaaren. "See Here, Mr. Walker." *Modern Screen*. May, 1944,
pp 40-41, 98-100.

A fast-paced synopsis of Robert Walker's life, including his marriage
to Jennifer Jones, their simultaneous rise to stardom and sudden marriage
trouble, which neither would talk about.

B105  Posner, Caryl. "The Mystery of Jennifer Jones." *Photoplay*. April,
1958,  pp  53, 80, 82, 84.

Published as *A Farewell to Arms* was being released nationally, this
extremely well-written and intelligent article traces the life of Jennifer Jones
right up to the film's making, closely examining her personal sorrows and
triumphs.

B106  Pritchett, Florence. "Pecking Away at Greg." *Silver Screen*.
November, 1946,  pp  30-31, 68-70.

A nicely-written profile of Gregory Peck that brings him up to his
most current film, *Duel in the Sun*. He says making the film was an enjoyable
experience, but most enjoyable was working with Jennifer Jones, an actress,
he says, who has "discovered the great secret of giving of herself, both as a
person, and as an actress."

B107  Pritchett, Florence. "Please Get Me Straight." *Silver Screen*. July,
1945,  pp  22-23, 71.

A pleasant interview with Robert Walker in which Jennifer Jones is not
mentioned once; however, at one point, he does say that he wishes his sons
had taken more after their mother.

B108  Pritchett, Florence. "Portrait of Jenny." *Photoplay*.  February, 1949,
pp  62, 107-08.

A typical fan magazine article that stresses the good points of Jennifer
Jones's character, from mother love, to a dedication to her craft. There are a
few amusing anecdotes from filming *Portrait of Jennie* (pre-dawn skating
lessons before shooting a certain sequence), but, otherwise, a long list of
compliments which obviously pleased the Selznick office.

B109  "Resolutions." *Movie Stars Parade*. January, 1946, pp 60-61.

Lauren Bacall, Laraine Day, Ginny Sims and Jennifer Jones list their
resolutions for the new year as they pertain to beauty care.  Jennifer vows to
"take a refresher even during the busiest days."

B110  St. Johns, Adela Rogers. "Who is Bernadette?" *Photoplay*. June,

1944, pp  34, 104-105.

Miss St. Johns examines the Jones/Walker divorce in light of Jennifer's association with Saint Bernadette, and asks several pertinent questions. Since Jennifer *is* Bernadette in the public's mind, does she owe anything to the dream of comfort and inspiration that she gave to a country at war? What was the right choice for her to make when forced to choose between her own portrayal of the little French saint and her personal marriage break-up? Did she pledge herself to an off-screen life similar to Bernadette's when she accepted the role?  The answer Miss St. Johns gives to these questions is a resounding  No.  The article is extremely interesting in showing how stars of past eras were expected to live up to their screen image.

B111 "Saintly Heroine." *Silver Screen*.  May, 1943,  p. 37.

An announcement (accompanied by three large photos) that "unknown" Jennifer Jones, a Selznick discovery with "limited experience," has won the role of Bernadette Soubirous. Includes a brief commentary on the gamble Fox is taking by giving such an important role to an unknown.

B112 "Salute." *Movie Stars Parade*.  April, 1944, p.  12.

A regular feature which "salutes" stars whose selfless actions are deemed worthy of mention.  Jennifer Jones is here recognized for graduating from a Nurse's Aid course without fanfare; in fact, no one even knew she was taking the course...

B113 "Star Keepsake." *Movie Stars Parade*.  June, 1928.  pp 26-27.

An interesting, brief profile of the actress who was "left bewildered and unsure of herself" by sudden stardom.  The article confirms Jennifer Jones's reputation for extreme shyness and claims her close friends are few.

B114 Stark, John.  "At 320 Pounds, Divine Teams with Tab Hunter in
       Bushwhack Western." *People*.  July 16, 1984.

A profile of actor/female impersonator Divine, as publicity for his upcoming film, *Lust in the Dust*, a title which, as Stark explains, is an in-joke, a film-buff reference to Jennifer Jones's 1946 *Duel in the Sun*, which was nicknamed "Lust in the Dust," and Stark offers some trivia as to how it got the nickname.  Divine is quoted as saying he's always being compared to Jennifer Jones, but admits to catching himself in the mirror and seeing Hedy Lamarr!

B115 "Tall Skinny Papa." *Modern Screen*.  April, 1945, pp 40-41, 84-88.

An interesting treatment of the Robert Walker story, concentrating on his weekday film work and Sunday visits with his two sons. His marriage to Jennifer is occasionally mentioned, but no attempt is made to analyze their problems.

B116 "The Cover." *Motion Picture*. June, 1947, p. 21.

A lovely portrait of Jennifer graces the cover of this issue, and the brief inside article gives few details of the "cover girl," but does mention some of her films roles.

B117 "Their Views on Love." *Photoplay*. November, 1943.

Six actressses, including Julie Bishop, Barbara Stanwyck and Jennifer Jones, were asked their views on "this thing called love." Jennifer advised readers not "to fool or experiment" with love, that marriage and life would "test it." It's intertesting that she would be asked to share her views on love at a time her marriage was falling apart... but that was still a secret.

B118 Wade, Jack. "The Woman Nobody Knows." *Modern Screen*. February, 1949, pp  44, 82, 84.

A well-written article detailing the private life of Jennifer Jones as if Wade had observed the actress's every move. Wade also relates several amusing incidents from the filming of *We Were Strangers* (1949).

B119 Walker, Michael. "Jennifer Jones." *Film Dope*. December, 1983, pp 29-30.

Very brief, choppy biography, covering only milestones of Jennifer Jones's life. Followed by filmography. A long endnote does offer some intelligent analysis, and the Selznick influence on her life and career is also mentioned.

B120 Watters, Susan. "Eye." *Women's Wear Daily*. March 7, 1980,  p. 4.

Following a state dinner at the White House with 140 attendees, Jennifer Jones is busy searching for her husband, but she has time to wax enthusiatic about First Lady Rosalyn Carter's mental health program, and also to praise several contemporary actresses, among them Sally Kellerman, who is heading for that "big break."

B121 "We Point With Pride." *Silver Screen*. May, 1944, p. 58.

A monthy feature spotlighting stars who accomplish something special on screen. This month, Jennifer Jones is singled out from the cast of *Since*

*You Went Away* and praised for dispelling the fear that she was a "one-picture phenomenon" and for proving herself to be a "truly great artist."

B122  Wilson, Elizabeth. "Girl Meets Vision." *Liberty.* September 25, 1943, pp 16-17, 72.

An entertaining article that explains Fox's decision to film Franz Werfel's book, *Song of Bernadette*, their search for a Bernadette, and their signing of Jennifer Jones after she looked at a stick and saw a vision. Several details from Jennifer's background are also included.

B123  Wilson, Elizabeth. "Quite a Change for Our Jennifer." *Silver Screen.* July, 1945, pp 24-25, 76.

Wilson visited the set of *Duel in the Sun*, recorded her observations, and later caught up with Jennifer Jones in the commissary. Interesting for a behind-the-scenes look at the filming, although it is written in a casual, chatty style that is sometimes annoying. The "change" for Jennifer is going from "saint to sinner," but Jones defends the promiscuous Pearl Chavez, whom she says isn't a bad girl, only "an exciting girl."

B124  Zeitlan, Ida. "Jenny Made up her Mind." *Modern Screen.* February, 1945, pp 42-43, 110-113.

A lengthy profile of Jennifer Jones (who was in the middle of filming *Love Letters*) that reveals several intimate details of the actress's life: a childhood wish that her eyes were brown, a hatred of dripping faucets, a habit of walking after dinner, etc. It is said that she will talk openly about Robert Walker, but not about their separation.

## NEWSPAPER ARTICLES

B125  "Babes in Hollywood." *The New York Times.* March 14, 1943.

Calls Jennifer Jones and Robert Walker the "luckiest young couple in Hollywood," and presents their marriage as a happy one. The details of their rise to fame are here too, but riddled with errors, i.e., Selznick is said to have first seen Jones in the Chicago production of *Claudia*.

B126  Benson, Walter. "Why Did She Do It?" *The National Enquirer.* December 31, 1967.

A disappointing examination of the Jennifer Jones suicide attempt on November 9, 1967. Financial difficulty and a decline of screen offers are ruled out, leaving loneliness as the reason. Her acting career is briefly summarized, and Benson makes the strange statement that neither Walker nor Selznick had had much confidence in her acting ability and were surprised by her success.

B127 Bernstein, Jonathan. "Actress Who Once Tried Suicide Gives $Million to Fight Mental Illness." *The National Enquirer.* January 22, 1980.

Title tells all. Relates Jennifer's interest in the treatment of mental illness and her large donation to the cause.

B128 Bracker, Milton. "Portrait of a Stage-Struck Lady." *The New York Times.* December 19, 1954.

Jennifer Jones reveals in this interview that the stage has always been her first love, but still feels loyal to Hollywood. Bracker terms this a "strong, apparently sincere, and even painful" alternation of loyalties. She comments on her upcoming Broadway debut in *Portrait of a Lady* and explains how she happened to be offered the part.

B129 Cameron, Kate. "Bernadette Star New to Screen." *The New York Daily News.* January 16, 1944.

In spite of claiming that Jennifer Jones had never appeared on the screen before, the artricle is an interesting profile of the actress and a record of how *Song of Bernadette* happened to be filmed.

B130 Cameron, Kate. "Jennifer Jones Comes Back to Screen in Two Pictures." *The New York Daily News.* May 18, 1952.

The two pictures mentioned are *Carrie* and *The Wild Heart,* but in this casual interview she talks mostly about her other films. She seems a little ashamed of her performance in *Madame Bovary,* explaining that she was "rushed while making it." She also mentions her next acting challenge, King Vidor's *Ruby Gentry.*

B131 Collins, Nancy. "A Song of Jennifer." *The Louisville Courier-Journal.* November 6, 1977.

Jennifer Jones is interviewed while in Washington, D.C. as a commissioner on the Huntington's Disease Council, and candidly talks about her life as Mrs. Norton Simon, her newly acquired appreciation of art, and her relationship with David O. Selznick. In looking back over her life, she remarks "I can hardly believe it's me."

B132 Cook, Alton. "Look, Ma -- I'm Acting! is not for Jennifer." *The New York World Telegram.* August 23, 1955.

A pleasant article about the parents of Jennifer Jones visiting the set of *Good Morning, Miss Dove*, and the actress not wanting them to see her in "old lady" make-up.

B133  Cook, Alton. "The Future Looks Mighty Bright for Jennifer." *The New York World Telegram*. January 20, 1944.

Written in praise of Jennifer's performance as Bernadette, overcoming odds that Fox executives would lose on their gamble of giving the role to an unknown. Cook says that marriage trouble is the only cloud on the horizon for the young star.

B134  D'Antonio, Dennis. "Most Beautiful Woman in the World is 57-year-old Actress Jennifer Jones." *The National Enquirer*. January 18, 1977.

Three beauty experts -- Carrie White, George Masters and Vidal Sassoon -- all agree and explain their reasons for bestowing this title on the former actress.

B135  Donovan, Katherine. "Jennifer Jones Refuses to Let Career Rule Personal Life." *The Boston Sunday Advertiser Pictorial Review*. March 26, 1944.

A fascinating editorial praising Jennifer Jones for risking her career to break up a marriage "where love no longer prevailed." In Donovan's estimation, Miss Jones is a woman of great courage, being sincere and individualistic despite the studio's expectations.

B136  Dowd, Maureen. "Is Jack Kemp Mr. Right?" *The New York Times*. June 28, 1987.

An interview with presidential candidate Kemp in which he says Jennifer Jones is his favorite actress and says he named a daughter in her honor.

B137  Dullea, Georgia. "Han Suyin's Many-Splendored World." *The New York Times*. January 25, 1985.

An interview with 68-year-old Han Suyin (who authored the book on which the Jennifer Jones film, *Love is a Many-Splendored Thing*, was based) who bemoans the fact that 30 years after the film was made, she is still identified with Jennifer Jones and the film's theme song. "I do get bored," she says, "because I have done other things."

B138  Finnigan, Joseph. "Jennifer Jones Returns to Movies after Three

Years with New Approach." *The Louisville Courier-Journal.* July 23, 1961.

A United Press story that announces Jennifer's return to motion pictures as Nicole Diver in *Tender is the Night.* In an interview, she reveals that she tried a new dramatic style in the film and is anxious to see how effective it will be. She won't explain what the new style is, but predicts the film will be "a turning point in my career." (Unfortunately, the film was not a success and she has made only three films since.)

B139 Graham, Sheila. "Jennifer Jones Calmly Looks Ahead." *The New York World Telegram.* October 25, 1965.

Interviewed while in London filming *The Idol,* Jennifer Jones talks about her sons, the failure of *Tender is the Night* (a good film in script form) and her future acting plans (a film based on the life of Aimee Semple McPherson).

B140 Harmetz, Aljean. "Coming to Terms with Success." *The New York Times.* April 8, 1984.

A lengthy article profiling director James Brooks, nominated as Best Director for *Terms of Endearment.* Harmetz tells how Brooks came to direct the film, first trying to adapt it as a vehicle for Jennifer Jones, then pursuading Paramount to buy the rights from Jones and her husband, Norton Simon.

B141 Hopper, Hedda. "All Talk With Jennifer Revolves Around Bob." *The Baltimore Sun.* April 25, 1943.

A pleasant profile of Jennifer Jones. There are very few quotes, but Miss Hopper describes her with rich detail. Her marriage to Robert Walker is pictured as being happy and healthy.

B142 Hopper, Hedda. "Meet Miss Jones." *The Chicago Sunday Tribune.* March 2, 1947.

Not a typical gossip column entry, this is an interesting look at stardom and how fans are affected by the performances of their favorite stars. The career of Jennifer Jones as it applies to this theme is analyzed with great skill, and Miss Hopper's conclusion is that Jennifer does not fit the mold. To many people she is still identified with Saint Bernadette, and to portray the radically different Pearl Chavez would have damaged many a star's career, but Jennifer seems to have been unscathed. As a bonus, there is a brief interview with Jones in which she explains this phenomenon.

B143  Hyams, Joe. "Jennifer Jones -- Not One for Words." *The New York Herald Tribune*. January 16, 1962.

A casual interview during which Jones begs not to be interviewed. Nevertheless, Hyams does coax a few interesting comments from Miss Jones.

B144  Hyams, Joe. "This is London." *The New York Herald Tribune*. May 16, 1956.

Jennifer Jones is interviewed on the set of *The Barretts of Wimpole Street*, but refuses to talk about *anything*. Hyams mentions that Miss Jones made several clever and interesting remarks, always followed by the comment, "off the record." Most stars who would adopt such an aloof attitude toward the press wouldn't be treated very well in print, but Hyams writes about Jones with respect and admiration.

B145  "Jennifer Jones has Everything." *The Portland Journal Sun*. October 3, 1943.

What Jennifer Jones has, according to this article, is a spiritual face that needs no glamorizing. The article is intended as publicity for *Song of Bernadette*, a role for which she will wear no make-up, and ends with Jennifer passing along her beauty tips.

B146  "Jennifer Jones Trying New Dramatic Style." *The New York Morning Telegraph*. July 19, 1961.

Jennifer Jones discusses her latest role in the soon-to-be-released *Tender is the Night*, and refers to a mysterious "new approach" to acting which she compares to religion. She makes the prophetic statement that if her new technique doesn't work, she fears she will be "finished in pictures."

B147  "Jennifer's Big Night." *The New York Post*. September 13, 1985.

Society columnist Suzy reports that Jennifer Jones will be honored by the University of Pennsylvania's nursing school for her efforts to "promote a fairer, more compassionate society."

B148  "Jennifer's Up There; So's Bob." *The Milwaukee Journal*. July 11, 1943.

A brief re-telling of the story of Jennifer Jones and Robert Walker, their romance and "good fortune" to be given film contracts at the same time. Facts seem accurate, and there's even a mention of their first try at Hollywood in 1939.

B149  "Jennifer's Wedding Party was all at Sea -- and Rough."  *The Daily Mirror*.  June 1, 1971.

Relates the amusing details of the Jennifer Jones/Norton Simon wedding which was performed at sea at 4a.m.

B150  McCrary, Tex and Jinx Falkenburg.  "New York Close-Up."  *The New York Herald Tribune*.  May 18, 1952.

Gives some interesting behind-the-scenes details from the filming of *Ruby Gentry*, and also some information on how she prepared for her hip-swinging role in *Duel in the Sun*.  Includes an interesting observation from Constance Collier on Jennifer's potential as a stage actress, and Jennifer's prediction of how she would react to unflattering theatre reviews.

B151  Masters, George.  "The Masters Touch."  *The New York Daily News*.  April 6, 1969.

Masters, make-up consultant for scores of Hollywood stars, discusses his professional relationship with Jennifer Jones, relating such details as her make-up preferences.  He says her figure is one of the most beautiful he has ever seen.

B152  Miller, John J.  "Millerdramas."  *The New York Inquirer*.  September 10, 1956.

Miller relates an incident that has not appeared in any other print source:  that when Jennifer Jones was in Hollywood in 1939, a producer tried to drive her back to his apartment, but she wrestled free and jumped out of the moving car, shaken up but unhurt.

B153  Miskin, Leo.  "About the Book, Mr. Houseman."  *The New York Morning Telegraph*.  February 29, 1972.

A fascinating article, actually written as an open letter to Mr. Houseman following the publishing of his book, *Run-Through*.  In the book, Houseman apparently mentions directing Jennifer Jones in *Hello, Out There* in 1943, and says that Selznick had given her the name "Jennifer Jones." Miskin takes Houseman to task over that statement.  A New York employee of David O. Selznick at the time Phylis Isley was hired, Miskin tells *his* version of how she got her screen name. He also includes an amusing tale of two rival New York newspaper reporters and their differing stories about Selznick's "newest discovery."

B154  Mosby, Aline.  "Jennifer Jones Speaks Out."  *The New York Times*.  March 30, 1955.

Jones does indeed "speak out" and denies that Selznick interferes with the production of her films. She also mentiones the recent failure of *Portrait of a Lady* in New York, calling it the "real failure of my life."

B155 Packard, Eleanor. "Tearful Jennifer, Selznick Desert 'Arms,' Head for NY." *The New York Daily News*. April 7, 1957.

Selznick and Jennifer Jones take a "surprise flight" to New York from Italy early on in the production of *A Farewell to Arms*, leaving everyone wondering what will happen next. Rumor is that the production will be dropped.

B156 Peper, William. "Jennifer Jones Eyes Return to the Stage." *The New York World Telegraph and Sun*. January 19, 1962.

An interview in which Jennifer Jones reveals that she is looking for a stage role, that she wants to "really develop as a stage actress," which was her first ambition.

B157 Pristin, Terry and Stephen Braun. "The Norton Simon Museum: Industrialist Reported Resting; His Decision Stirs Speculation." *The Los Angeles Times*. March 10, 1989.

Details Simon's decision to turn over the control of his museum, which houses a renowned collection of valuable paintings, to his wife, Jennifer Jones. Several of his friends venture their opinion of how well Jones can manage the museum and whether or not the collection will remain intact, and in Pasadena.

B158 Rosenfield, John. "From Nobody to Star in a Few Short Hours." *The Dallas Morning News*. March 5, 1944.

Praises Jennifer for her Oscar-winning performance as Saint Bernadette, and adds a little local flavor (her parents live in Dallas).

B159 Rosenfield, John. "Passing Show." *The Dallas Morning News*. May 26, 1949.

A thoughtful editorial on Jennifer Jones, praising her talent, but criticizing Selznick for not allowing her to be seen on the screen more often, in at least in three or four films per year.

B160 Sarris, Andrew. *The Village Voice*. May 18, 1982.

In an untitled column, Sarris refutes the school of thought that Jones would be an inappropriate choice to portray the demented Jean Harris, the subject of Diana Trilling's book on the Scarsdale Diet creator's murder. He points out that Jones has killed people in three movies, committed suicide in one and engaged in adultery in seven.

B161  Scott, Vernon. "Art Fills Life of Film Beauty." *The Sunday Record.* September 15, 1974.

Jennifer Jones, in the middle of making *The Towering Inferno*, talks candidly about her return to films, her life as Mrs. Norton Simon, and her newly-acquired appreciation of art.

B162  "Selznick, it Seems, Knew His Jennifer Jones." *The New York Herald Tribune.* April 23, 1944.

Compliments Selznick for having faith in Jennifer Jones, his newest discovery who has more than justified his interest and faith in her. Mentions his latest plans for Jones -- a pivotal role in *Since You Went Away.*

B163  Skolsky, Sidney. "Hollywood is My Beat..." *The New York Post Magazine.* January 28, 1962.

A choppy biography of Jennifer Jones, sprinkled with quotes about her role in *Tender is the Night*, her views on acting techniques, and her interest in yoga.

B164  Skolsky, Sidney. "Jennifer's Scared by Bernadette." *The New York Post.* July 24, 1943.

Brief profile of the actress who has been signed to portray Bernadette which makes no effort to hide certain facts, i.e., her two previous films. Jennifer is "scared" of seeing the rushes, preferring instead to see the completed film.

B165  "*The Song of Bernadette.*" *The New York Herald Tribune.* April 9, 1944.

Compares Jennifer Jones to Vivien Leigh, Greer Garson and Marie Dressler as an actress who will be forever identified with a particular role. In Jennifer's case, it is predicted that she will be associated with the "spirit of Easter" in the minds of millions.

B166  Sullivan, Kay. "Portrait of Jennifer." *Parade.* April 11, 1948.

Sullivan writes that Jennifer Jones is an example of something rare in Hollywood -- an actress who has remained the same "quiet, serious and shy girl" she was when she first arrived in Hollywood. According to Sullivan, Jones is not Hollywood's idea of what a star should be, preferring instead to live a quiet life at home with her two sons.

B167 Tallmer, Jerry. "A Fast Boat to the Altar." *The New York Post Magazine.* June 6, 1971.

A lengthly profile of Norton Simon which begins and ends with Jennifer Jones, first by relating the details of their wedding at sea, and concluding with a short synopsis of Miss Jones's life.

B168 Thompson, Howard. "Presenting the Lady Called Jones." *The New York Times.* May 25, 1952.

A slight but insightful interview in which Jennifer Jones remarks on directors (no two work alike), the soon-to-be-released *The Wild Heart* (hopeful of the results) and her maturity as an actress (made *Bernadette* without knowing what was "going on half the time").

B169 Watts, Stephen. "Miss Jones Looks at Love in London." *The New York Times.* December 5, 1965.

An interesting interview in which Jennifer Jones talks more than usual. She denies that *The Idol* (which she is currently filming) is her come-back, explains why she decided to make the film (she had been the original choice, but had turned it down), and comments on how it feels to be acting after a three-year hiatus.

B170 "When Miss Isley Washed Her Hair." *The New York Herald Tribune.* July 23, 1944.

A publicity story for *Since You Went Away* that recounts Jennifer Jones's amusing cab ride to Manhattan from Long Island, her wet hair dangling out the window.

## ADDITIONAL PRINT SOURCES

The following articles (alphabetized by title) were found in the Jennifer Jones clipping file at the Wisconsin Center for Film and Research in Madison. Unfortunately, the publication's name and date had been obliterated, and although every effort was made to obtain the missing information, the titles do not appear in the standard bibliographic sources.

B171 "Discoveries of the Month."

A brief profile of Jennifer Jones, obviously from early 1944, that is interesting because it not only admits that she has made films before *Song of Bernadette*, but names the studio and one of her leading men (John Wayne).

B172 "The Editor's Page."

An open letter (signed by Delight Evans) to Jennifer Jones congratulating her on winning the Oscar for her "beautiful, deeply stirring performance" as Bernadette Soubirous.  Evans calls Jones a very lucky girl for winning the coveted award for her first picture, while her Oscar co-winner, Paul Lukas, had to wait years for his award.  Evans also congratulates Ingrid Bergman for being a gracious loser, but predicts that her Oscar has been merely "postponed."

B173  "Find of '42."

An entertaining little article about an actress brand new on the film scene, a Selznick discovery named Jennifer Jones.  Her face is said to resemble Maureen O'Sullivans -- "Starry-eyed, elfin and gentle" -- and she is said to have the figure of a "long-legged seraph."  According to the uncredited author, Selznick signed her to play Nora in *Keys of the Kingdom*, after she failed to convince him she was the perfect *Claudia*, and it is predicted that she will make an indelible impression in this, her "first motion picture experience."  "Jennifer Jones" is said to be her real name, and it is also said that her father named her after a pet calf!

B174  "Jennifer Jones."

A brief biographical sketch of Jennifer Jones followed by a series of interesting pictures from her life. There are snapshots of her as a child and candids from various periods of her life, from homelife with Robert Walker, to attending a preview with Watson Webb. There are also stills of her film highlights.

B175  "Jennifer on Fashion."

A brief article published in England while she was there filming *The Wild Heart* that reveals her behind-the-scenes actions during the filming.  She apparently became quite a favorite with the residents of Shropshire, where the crew was shooting on location.  Includes a listing of her favorite clothing styles (short evening dresses) and jewelry (pearl necklaces and earrings).

B176  "Jennifer's Just 'Mom' to her Boys."

Written by Ed Wallace, this disarming article was obviously written for a New York publication just prior to her Broadway debut in *Portrait of a Lady*.  A few trivial details are offered (her height, her favorite foods) before Wallace settles into a humorous vein, recounting the difficulty Jennifer and David Selznick had finding a suitable name for their daughter.  When asked what she would like to change about her two boys, she replies that she would rather they address her as mother "instead of 'mom'."

B177  "The Miracle of Jennifer."

Maxine Arnold (who also wrote several articles for *Photoplay* about Jennifer Jones) here frankly and entertainly discusses Jennifer's childhood, and being from Tulsa herself, knows just what it was like to grow up there. She also writes that *Song of Bernadette* was not Jennifer's first film, and devotes three paragraphs to her unhappy experience at Republic Studio in 1939. This is interesting because *Bernadette* had not yet been released, and writing about her previous film work was supposed to be forbidden.

B178  "Song of Jennifer."

A short poem written in praise of Jennifer Jones. It has no rhyme, but lots of charm and manages to weave several details from her early life, marriage to Robert Walker and even a few film achievements into its verse.

B179  "Story of a Shy Girl."

Written by Kate Holliday, this is one of the better early articles about Jennifer Jones, thoroughly covering the actress's life with warmth and fascinating detail. Her shyness, acting aspirations and romance with Robert Walker are professionally and interestingly presented. Rather long, but well worth reading.

B180  "Thanks, Hollywood -- Says Jennifer Jones."

A fascinating an important article, a letter ostensibly written by Jennifer, thanking everyone who contributed to her award-winning performance as Bernadette Soubirous. Jennifer writes with humility and grace and admits that seeing the faces of Bette Davis, Jean Arthur, Ingrid Bergman and Claudette Colbert as she made her way to the stage to accept her Oscar made her feel unworthy of the award. She touches on several important issues -- the fear that she would be known as a "one picture girl," the fear of being "typed," and the fear that success has "come a little early perhaps." She mentions the flood of congratulatory telegrams following her Oscar win, (including one from actress Michele Morgan), but says none meant more to her than Henry Kings's.

B181  "Unhappy Ending."

The by-line is Avery Carroll's, but the genuine sadness that comes through this article as it tells how the fairy tale romance of Robert Walker and Jennifer Jones was shattered, was apparently felt by a whole generation. The clock had struck midnight and the "Cinderella Couple" had broken up. The story of their courtship is perhaps romanticized a bit, but wartime America wanted -- and needed -- to believe in fairy tales.

B182  "We Present."

A short biographical summary that reveals the facts as well as a few trivial details, i.e., clothing preference is feminine styles in pastel colors, doesn't like hats, first crush was a red-haired choir boy.

# Appendix A: Robert Walker Obituary

From *The New York Times*, August 30, 1951

## ACTOR WALKER DIES AFTER DRUG DOSAGE

Breathing of Film Star Stops When Doctors Use Sedative in Emotional Crisis

By Gladwin Hall

LOS ANGELES, Aug. 29 -- Robert Walker, 32-year-old film star whose own desparate and protracted struggle with dark emotional forces topped any of his conflicts on the screen, died last night while undergoing medical treatment for the latest of many tragic crises in his life.

The actor, who attracted national attention in December, 1948, when he fled from a Topeka, Kan., psychiatric clinic and smashed up the local police station after being arrested for drunkenness, succumbed to what was reported as a "respiratory failure" after receiving a sedative injection at his Sunset Boulevard home in suburban Brentwood.

Dr. Frederick J. Hacker, a psychiatrist who had been treating Mr. Walker for eighteen months, said he had been called about 6p.m. by the actor's housekeeper and found him in "a highly emotional state."

He kept saying, "I feel terrible, Doc -- do something, quick," the psychiatrist reported, adding that he did not know whether the actor had been drinking.

### Drug Is Administered

After two hours' pleading failed to calm Mr. Walker, Dr. Hacker said he called Dr. Sidney Silver to administer sodium amytal, which "we had given him twenty-five to thirty times in the past without ill effects."

A seven-and-one-half grain dose was given, Dr. Hacker said, only a fraction of previous doses the actor had received, but almost immediately he turned blue and gradually stopped breathing -- a reaction which, Dr. Silver said, occurred only about once in 10,000 cases.  He certified the death as natural, due to respiratory failure.

Dr. Victor Cefalu, assistant county coroner, said today that a fifteen-grain dose of the drug could be toxic, and that the drug accumulated in the system.  The coroner's office said there would be no autopsy unless a member of the family requested it.

Mr. Walker, whose career as a star in a score of pictures had been concentrated in a brief eight years, only last Saturday had completed work in the Helen Hayes film "My Son John" at Paramount studios and had been reported in an apparently cheerful mood.

His death cut short what had been regarded as a successful comeback from a severe psychological crackup.

This manifested itself in 1945, when he was divorced after a marriage of six years by Jennifer Jones, the film actress, who subsequently became the wife of David O. Selznick, film producer.

### Vanished During Film

Although at that time, only two years after his debut in "Bataan," he was making $100,000 a year according to the divorce testimony, the actor suddenly disappeared in the midst of the filming of "See Here, Private Hargrove," and was located only after two days.

A year later he was arrested for hit-and-run driving in Beverly Hills and fined $500.  In July, 1948, he married Barbara Ford, daughter of John Ford, the producer-director, but they separated after five weeks and she subsequently obtained an annulment.

Shortly after their separation, he was arrested for drunken driving, and his treatment at the Menninger Clinic in Topeka became known with his outburst there.   However, he left the clinic in May, 1949, reported completely readjusted, and returned to Hollywood to resume his film career.

Though Dr. hacker said that the actor's psychiatric difficulties dated back to 1943, it was generally supposed (and occasional comments of Mr. Walker himself lent substance to this) that his separation from Miss Jones had precipitated his distress.

They had two children, Robert, 11, and Michael, 10, who had been visiting the actor this summer, but who were away from the home visiting friends when Mr. Walker died.

### Returned to Hollywood

Since his return to Hollywood, the actor had played in "Vengeance Valley" at Metro-Goldwyn-Mayer studios, where he was under contract, and, on loan, in "Strangers on a Train" at Warner Brothers before his recent Paramount assignment.  Leo McCarey, producer and director of the last picture, said:

"I have worked closely with Bob during these past few months and learned to know him as both a fine gentleman and a great actor.  We had our final working session together only last Saturday.  At that time he showed no indication of being in ill health.  On the contrary, he did his final recording with great zest.  I had just run the rough-cut of the picture for him, and, although a modest fellow, he fairly beamed at the results."

His films also included "Madame Curie," "See Here, Private Hargrove," "Since You Went Away," "Thirty Seconds Over Tokyo," "Till the Clouds Roll By," and "Sea of Grass."

He was the son of Horace Walker, Salt Lake City newspaper editor, who is flying here with Mrs. Walker.  The actor attended the San Diego Army and Navy Military Academy, the Pasadena (Calif.) Playhouse dramatic school and the Academy of Dramatic Arts in New York.

After an unproductive stage debut in Greenwich Village, he did radio work in Tulsa, Okla., and in New York, where his voice attracted the attention of Hollywood scouts.

# *Appendix B: David O. Selznick Obituary*

From *The New York Times*, June 23, 1965.

**DAVID O. SELZNICK, 63, PRODUCER OF *'GONE WITH THE WIND*,' DIES**

HOLLYWOOD, June 22 -- David O. Selznick, one of the leading producers in the motion picture industry, died of a coronary occlusion this afternoon at Mount Sinai Hospital.

Mr. Selznick, who was 63 years old, was stricken in the office of his lawyer, Barry Brannan, in Beverly Hills, and was rushed to the hospital. His wife, Jennifer Jones, the actress, was with him at the time of the attack.

Mr. Selznick, who produced "Gone With the Wind," the movies' biggest money-maker, and his wife had returned to their Beverly Hills home last week after spending three months in New York City.

Mercurial, shrewd, self-confident and enormously gifted, David O. Selznick climed to the pinnacle of power and success in Hollywood with films that are now classics and actors who are considered screen immortals.

His films included "Intermezzo," "Rebecca," "David Copperfield," "Little Women," "The Prisoner of Zenda," "Dinner at Eight," "A Star is Born," "Duel in the Sun," and the epic, "Gone With the Wind."

He was instrumental in spurring the careers of such actors as Clark Gable, Vivien Leigh, Ingrid Bergman, Joseph Cotten, Gregory Peck, Katharine Hepburn, Joan Fontaine, Fred Astaire, Leslie Howard, Myrna Loy and his wife, Miss Jones.

Mr. Selznick, a 6-foot 1-inch, 200-pounder, moved quickly, spoke rapidly and worked tirelessly. He produced quality films with three trademarks: top stars, the finest writers and no expense spared.

Even in the twilight of his career, he remained wide-eyed and even brash, although a trace of pessimism and melancholy became apparent in recent years.

"Nothing in Hollywood is permanent," Mr. Selznick said in 1959 on a Hollywood set, as Tara, the mansion built for "Gone With the Wind," was being dismembered and shipped to Atlanta. Ga. "Once photographed, life here is ended. It is almost symbolic of Hollywood. Tara has no rooms inside. It was just a facade. So much of Hollywood is a facade."

Mr. Selznick spoke in quick, staccato sentences. While working on a film, he virtually exhausted himself, laboring round-the-clock, seeking perfection to the minutest detail and stubbornly insisting on his own ideas.

### Fighting Perfectionist

As a producer, Mr. Selznick was preoccupied with quality, and his perfectionism led him to many fights with directors.

"Gone With the Wind" started with George Cukor directing. He was replaced by Victor Fleming.

"A Farewell to Arms" saw a classic feud between Mr. Selznick and John Huston. "It was a case of one Alp and two Hannibals," said Mr. Huston after he had been replaced in Italy by Charles Vidor.

"I asked for a vioilinist," Mr. Selznick shot back, "and, instead, in John, got a soloist."

As one of Hollywood's most famous memo writers, Mr. Selznick dictated more than 1.5 million words of memos to two exhausted stenographers during the filming of "Gone With the Wind." At one point, he sent a message to Vivien Leigh that weighed half a pound and took the actress 10 days to reply to.

Mr. Selznick was born in Pittsburgh, on May 10, 1902, the son of Lewis J. Selznick, a Russian immigrant, who had earned and lost a fortune in the movie business.

With unbounded confidence in the abilities of his two sons, Myron and David, the elder Selznick spared little expense in rearing them as prodigals. Myron, who later became a Hollywood agent, was given an allowance of $1,100 a week at the age of 21. The younger, David, was given $300 a week at 18.

David Selznick attended public and private schools and, for a brief period, Columbia University. He developed an interest in filmmaking in his early teens.The Selznick family fortune was swept away in the stock market crash. L.J. (as he was called in Hollywood and New York), moved from a 22-room apartment on Park Avenue to three furnished rooms where Mrs. Selznick did the cooking. All the family possessions, including Mrs. Selznick's jewels, were sold.

### Job as Reader

With zest and self-confidence, the younger Selznick got his first movie job by cajoling Harry Rapf of Metro-Goldwyn-Mayer into hiring him, nominally as a reader of scripts at $100 a week at a two-week trial.

Mr. Rapf had initially protested. "Readers don't get that kind of money," he said.

"I know they don't," Mr. Selznick retorted. "But I'll do more for you than read scripts. I'll help you fix them. I'll write titles. I'll do everything that has to be done to them."

Mr. Rapf hired him. Within several weeks, Mr. Selznick's pay was doubled and he was given a permanent job. A few months later, his salary was increased to $300 and he was appointed Mr. Rapf's assistant on the production of the Tim McCoy western films.

Mr. Selznick next went to Paramount, offering himself on a similar trial arrangement. He received a $300 job and became an assistant to B.P. Schulberg, head of the studio, who had told him early:

"You're the most arrogant young man I've ever known."

In April, 1930, Mr. Selznick married Irene Mayer, Louis B. Mayer's younger daughter. Mr. Mayer, the head of MGM, was furious when the young Selznick courted his daughter. He even refused to speak to him at the wedding.

Shortly afterward, however, when the young man walked away from his job at Paramount, Mr. Mayer did have a few words to say to his new son-in-law.

"How dare you give up that contract," he yelled. "And you married to my daughter."

Mr. Selznick left Paramount to make films on his own, becoming vice president, in charge of all production at RKO-Radio. It was there that he started producing such quality films as "A Bill of Divorcement," to which he brought Katharine Hepburn and George Cukor, the director, to Hollywood; "The Animal Kingdom," with Ann Harding, and the famous "King Kong."

After planning "Little Women," Mr. Selznick left RKO to return to his father-in-law's studio, MGM, as vice president and head of his own production unit.

Mr. Selznick was greeted coolly by most of the executives there. Many felt he was using his relationship with Mr. Mayer to get ahead.

"The son-in-law also rises," became one of the gags around Hollywood at the time.

In an incident related by Bosley Crowther, film critic for The New York Times, in "The Lion's Share," Mr. Selznick was treated so coldly by MGM executives that, at one point, he went home, threw himself on the bed and cried.

His wife comforted him, "Let them yammer," she said. "You can still take the best that the studio has to work with. Serve your term and make some films!"

Mr. Selznick's early films at MGM included "Dinner at Eight," "Dancing Lady," and "Viva Villa." Freddie Bartholomew was discovered by the producer and made famous in "David Copperfield."

In 1935, the producer left MGM to form an independent company. He was backed by Cornelius V. Whitney, John Hay Whitney, his brother Myron, Robert and Arthur Lehman, the bankers, John Hertz and Irving Thalberg and Norma Shearer (Mrs. Thalberg). Mr. Selznick did not invest any money but he owned a little more than half of the company.

In the early summer of 1936, Mr. Selznick was busy with "The Garden of Allah," with Marlene Dietrich, when a wire reached him from Kay Brown, the New York story editor, urging him to buy the film rights to a new Civil War novel. It was "Gone With the Wind," by Margaret Mitchell, an unknown in the literary world.

At the time, the feeling in Hollywood was that the Civil War had been played out with "The Birth of a Nation." Mr. Selznick, however, was interested, although he had misgivings about the problems of producing a novel of such length (1,037 pages). Finally, the novel was purchased for $50,000.

As winter came and the sales of the novel soared, the reading public, spurred by Mr. Selznick's publicity, became interested in the cast of the film. Tallulah Bankhead, Norma Shearer and Bette Davis were mentioned for the leading role of Scarlett O'Hara.

So strong was the public interest that when Miss Shearer declined to play Scarlett, The New York Times regretted her decision in an editorial.

### Curfew on Memos

Vivien Leigh, a hazel-eyed brown-haired British actress, was finally chosen in almost typically dramatic fashion. In order to clear the studio's lot for the building of Tara, the movie plantation, a maze of old sets had to be removed. It was suggested that instead of tearing down the sets, they should be burned and used to represent the dramatic highlight of the film, the burning of Atlanta. Mr. Selznick agreed.

While the cameras were shooting the scene, and as flames rose in the studio's night sky, the producer felt a tug on his sleeve. He turned and saw his brother, Myron, accompanied by a beautiful girl.

"I want you to meet Scarlett O'Hara," Myron said dramatically. Mr. Selznick stared at Miss Leigh and promptly signed her for the role.

The picture went before the cameras officially on Jan. 26, 1938. During the 22 weeks of shooting, Mr. Selznick's work habits became legend. He worked at times at three-day stretches without sleep, feeding himself Benzadrine and thyroid extract and playing poker and roulette to relax.

His memos became more prolific. At one point Clark Gable, the film's Rhett Butler, was routed out of bed at 3a.m. by a messenger who presented him with a document - a memo on the portrayal of the role. Mr. Gable and the others finally revolted and established a 9p.m. curfew on memos.

At the time, the film was the most expensive ($4,250,000) and one of the longest (3 hours and 45 minutes) ever produced. It has since grossed in excess of $50 million and has been reissued several times.

In seeking Mr. Gable for the film, Mr. Selznick agreed to a financial arrangement with MGM, the star's studio, in which MGM put up half the production costs in return for a share in the film's profits.

"I have never regretted it," Mr. Selznick once said. "I wouldn't have made the movie without Clark."

At the peak of his career, Mr. Selznick was voted for 10 successive years as the No. 1 producer of box-office successes by motion-picture exhibitors of the country.

Despite this, Mr. Selznick was notably unsuccessful at times, in hiring top actors and producers. On receiving an overture from the producer, Nunnally Johnson wrote:

"I should certainly like to work for you, although my understanding of it is that an assignment from you consists of three months' work and six months of recuperation."

A Hollywood saying was, simply, "Selznick eats directors, writers and secretaries."

Since 1948, Mr. Selznick had been generally inactive in Hollywood, and in recent years had been involved in European film distribution, the sale of his films to television and several stage plays. None of the stage plays came to fruition.

In 1949, Mr. Selznick married Jennifer Jones and he became involved in the production of most of her recent films.

Miss Jones, who had been married to the late actor Robert Walker, had starred in several of Mr. Selznick's films, including "Duel in the Sun," and "Since You Went Away."

The producer and his wife lived in an elegantly rustic home on an estate atop a hill overlooking Beverly Hills. They also maintained an apartment at the Waldorf Towers in New York.

"Very few people have mastered the art of enjoying their wealth," Mr. Selznick remarked several months ago. "I have mastered that art and therefore I spend my time enjoying myself."

# Index

This index refers to page numbers as well as to entry codes in enumerated sections. Entries preceded by "A" can be found under Awards and Nominations, by "B" in the Bibliography, by "F" in the Filmography, and by "R" under Radio, Theatre, Television. Coded entry numbers are given only for the primary reference of an index item; secondary references are to page numbers whether or not they appear in enumerated sections. For page numbers of the enumerated chapters, refer to the table of contents.

## About the Author

JEFFREY L. CARRIER, employed by the creative department of Ogilvy & Mather Advertising, New York, compiled the filmography for the memoirs of silent film star Patsy Ruth Miller and has published articles on Blanche Sweet and Laura La Plante.